Wilder Ways

Wilder Ways

Donald C. Jackson

University Press of Mississippi • Jackson

www.upress.state.ms.us

The University Press of Mississippi is a member of the Association of American University Presses.

Manufactured in the United States of America

Earlier versions of "A Prescription for Treating Woods Rambling Syndrome," "We Do It Because," "Ditch Fishing," and "Rendering Southern Glue" were originally published in *Mississippi Wildlife.*

An earlier version of "Bristle-Face Cathedral" was originally published as "Passages Through Bristle-Face Cathedral" in *The Versatile Hunting Dog.*

First printing 2012

∞

Library of Congress Cataloging-in-Publication Data

Jackson, Donald C., 1951–
Wilder ways / Donald C. Jackson.
p. cm.
ISBN 978-1-61703-274-5 (cloth : alk. paper) — ISBN 978-1-61703-275-2 (eBook)
1. Hunting—United States—Anecdotes. 2. Outdoor life. 3. Wildlife-related recreation. 4. Hunting stories, American I. Title.
SK33.J226 2012
799.2—dc23 2011034267

British Library Cataloging-in-Publication Data available

To my grandfathers, Robert L. Harris and Robert A. Jackson,
whose love for hunting and fishing was passed along to me

Contents

Wilder Ways

Ditch Fishing

If there's a creek around, I've got to get in it. As a young un' in rural north-central Kentucky, when I was between seven and nine years old, I'd swim in them just as soon as snow and ice began to melt. The bite and the sparkle of cold water thrilled me. I'd come out blue and shaking and then sit in the sun on gravel bars or flat rocks as the wind dried me and the early spring sun tried to warm me. Later in the season I'd prowl among pools and riffles catching frogs and salamanders and marveling at the mystery of the secret corners full of moss and ferns and lurking woodland spirits.

We moved from Kentucky to Arkansas when I was ten years old. The switch from rural to suburban environments was tempered by the fact that there were woods and water near our Arkansas home that were within walking distance. And, behind the church where my father was serving as pastor, there was a little creek full of cobblestones. I'd sneak off from Sunday school and spend my hours catching crayfish. Time would slip away and, more Sundays than not, I'd find myself quietly entering the sanctuary of my father's church long after the worship service began. Folks, especially my parents, noticed when I'd drift in and take a seat in the back corner of the sanctuary, but little was said. They knew that I was nurturing my love for moving water, a love that has endured now for over sixty years.

As I moved through the chapters of high school and college, my range increased. I ventured into the Ozarks and discovered smallmouth bass fishing, trout fishing, and canoeing in the region's fabulous streams. My love for streams became an addiction. Wherever my ramblings led me, I was able to find creeks and creek fishing. From Alaska as a wilderness sojourner, through Asia and Africa as a Peace Corps volunteer, and then back to Kentucky during seminary, I nurtured spiritual connections with God and the rhythms of the earth that are only found on (and in) creeks.

Then, after graduate school and a post-doctoral assignment with the University of Alaska, I joined the wildlife and fisheries faculty at Mississippi State University. It was professionally the right move but it also was a tough move from a personal perspective. The search image I'd developed the previous thirty-five years regarding creeks, especially *fishable* creeks, simply didn't fit with the Mississippi landscape. From all that I could tell, most streams had been ripped apart by dredging and channelization projects under the guise of "flood control" and drainage of wetlands for agriculture, or scoured by gravel mining or killed by dams. When I'd drive across the state, I'd see lots of ditches but, from my vantage point on bridges, I couldn't find any evidence of "creeks."

I struggled mightily to shift my thoughts and to control the growing void in my trembling heart. I pretended that it didn't matter . . . that I didn't need creeks or creek fishing. I fished ponds and lakes and, from time to time, I'd travel over to Arkansas to fish highland creeks with some of my old friends. This worked for a while . . . sort of.

But, after three or four years of this game, I realized that something had to change. Either I was going to have to pull up roots and take a job someplace else where there were creeks to fish in, or I was going to have to find a way and a place to go creek fishing in Mississippi. To *not* go creek fishing was not an option.

Within twenty miles of my home I knew that there were three substantial bridges that crossed moving water. The places looked like ditches and accordingly had been written off by me as not worth messing with. But driven by desperation, I decided to go to them for a closer look . . . it sure couldn't hurt just to go look.

On my first foray to one of those ditches, I pulled my old truck over to a wide spot just beyond the bridge and, light spinning rod in hand, "waded" through the tall grass and weeds down the slope to the water. I was soaking wet from the dew by the time I got down to the ditch . . . and also relieved to have made it without getting snake bit.

I paused for a few moments, just to look around me and to let the morning slip via spiritual osmosis into my soul. It was a lovely morning. The sunlight was just starting to filter through the trees along the bank. It was softened by the thick, almost misty, air. Bird song from wood thrushes and indigo buntings filled the landscape with sweetness. The "tonking" of a rain crow (yellow-billed cuckoo) from a high perch overlooking the ditch reverberated through the forest.

The morning was very, very still. There was just a little chill in the air but that suited me just fine. Then I stepped out into flowing water. I was shocked by how cool the water was. Because I was only wearing old tennis shoes and a pair of cutoff jeans, it took a few moments to acclimate myself to the cool water. And, surprisingly, instead of sinking into soft substrate . . . mud and silt and heaven only knows what sort of filth . . . as I'd thought I would down there in that ditch, I found myself actually on a stable bottom that was mostly covered with small gravel. The water was also *amazingly* clear. I hadn't expected it to be that clear.

Upstream from where I stood, shadows from the forest along the banks of the ditch were still deep, and a little bit spooky, on the water. I could vaguely see through the shadows that the channel disappeared around a bend about a hundred yards away. That bend in the stream and the unknown beyond seemed to call my name. It is always this way with creeks. I just must go "one more bend" (one after another . . . after another).

I tied on a small spinner bait and started working my way against the current. The water swirled around my legs and tugged at me. I moved quietly and steadily upstream. Through the years I've learned that fishing in an upstream direction is generally best because the fish are not alerted by a drifting plume of silt from an angler's shuffling feet. As I moved forward, some old gears started clicking into place and the old self, the fisherman of creeks past, began to emerge from a sort of hibernation.

As I moved into those shadows beyond the bridge, I encountered the unexpected. Near the bridge, there had indeed been substantial channel work. There were few trees and the channel was straight and of uniform depth. Blackberries and other thorny brambles and vines ruled the stream bank. But beyond that short reach, just beyond the bend in the channel, the world changed. The straightness in the channel shifted to meanders. There were gravel bars and high cut banks. The water rippled across gravel and scoured deep green eddies downstream from old logs and roots. I cast into one of these deeper pockets, started the retrieve, and something slammed my lure. I pulled back on the little rod and the water from the eddy erupted in spray and sparkle as a bass went airborne. I could actually see the fish as it ripped around in the clear water. Then it made a circle across a shoal and plunged back into its deep hole below the log.

I kept the pressure on it with my tiny rod, got it to come back out of the hole, and eventually was able to get it close enough so that I could reach down, grab it by its lower jaw, and lift it from the water. It sparkled like a jewel, as indeed it was. I checked it closely and saw that it was a spotted ("Kentucky") bass, not a largemouth bass—a true "stream bass" in every sense of the word—the Mississippi equivalent of smallmouth bass but better suited for the warmer streams of the Deep South.

After releasing the fish, I just stood for a few moments looking at the water and how the channel twisted away into the woods. I really hadn't expected to find a place like this or fishing like this. The "ditch" below this Mississippi bridge was a ditch only for a short distance before it became a creek again. Once back in the woods and beyond the first bend beyond the trees, it became a series of riffles and pools and highly fishable water. *This* is what I'd been looking for. I was back in business as a creek fisherman!

After catching that first bass on the spinner bait, I took off the spinner and replaced it with a small silvery top-water lure called a Rapala. If this was indeed bass water, then I figured that I'd fish for them just like I'd fished for smallmouth bass in my old haunts up in the Ozarks.

I moved steadily upstream, reconnecting with a world and a way that rushed like a torrent through the emptiness that I'd lived with during the previous years. There was magic in the moving water. The tiny rod became an extension of the man, the angler, probing, teasing, enticing the bass in that creek to strut their stuff. They smashed the lure as it quivered and shimmered and darted across the water's surface. Most weighed less than a pound, but in their world, they were king pins, the top of the chain, and they acted accordingly. Occasionally I'd catch a largemouth bass that lurked in some backwater corner of the creek, or longear sunfish in a sunny spot where they'd grouped for nesting, but most of the fish that I caught were spotted bass, their brown backs, steely silver-blue sides, and faint stripes on cheeks giving them a regal appearance. Indeed, they were princes and princesses. They fought with valor befitting royalty. And I respected them accordingly. Those I managed to bring to hand were quickly unhooked and released because I knew, from long experience as an angler and as a professional fisheries biologist, that creek bass tend to be very slow growing. It takes a very long time to replace one that's removed from the creek. Creek bass populations simply are not the sort of fish stocks that are capable of sustaining very much (if any) consumptive exploitation. Rather, their value is in a different realm.

Creek bass like the ones I caught that day pull the angler into a world very much akin to that of squirrel hunters. They must be stalked carefully and quietly. Precision aim (casting) is required. And along the way, the angler fishing for bass in creeks (as with squirrel hunters in the October woods) lets the wild world flow into his senses. The creek bass angler pays attention to the way leaves move upon the water's surface and how currents swirl and twist. Shadows are used to advantage. Movements are steady, almost rhythmic. The creek angler must keep moving, but with deliberation, and pause often. This pausing is essential because the power and beauty of creek fishing is really founded on the angler becoming fully integrated with the flow and rhythm of the water and the surrounding environment . . . trying to see, to know, to understand this wild and vibrant world from the fish's perspective, to pay attention to small details . . . backwaters full of mussel tracks, raccoon tracks on sand bars, birds along the stream bank, birds *in* the stream . . . and to walk with caution around obstructions, ever watchful for snakes of all kinds, to use beams and shafts of sunlight as they penetrate the deeper pools revealing the positioning of the fish ahead, and then to engage in the final stalk, the cast, the settling of the lure, the moment of stillness . . . then the twitch, then another, perhaps a very slight tremor or shallow dive, followed by another moment of stillness . . . then THE EXPLOSION and the fight is on. It is the best of the best.

I caught several fine bass that first morning on that Mississippi creek. When I sloshed my way back downstream to the bridge and my truck, every fish I'd caught was firmly in the creel of my heart. The clear water over gravel, the green of the forest that draped over the creek, the bounding deer, the cruising moccasins, the turtles in splashes of sunlight on logs, the sparkle from riffles, bird calls, water striders, whirligig beetles, mayflies under rocks, caddisflies in their cases all over submerged wood, water willow doing a ballet in the current next to a gravel bar, a mink slipping quietly and with beady eyes along the moss-covered stream bank . . . all merged in synergy to produce an incredible mosaic that filled the void that had been growing in my heart.

I declared myself guilty of failure to probe beyond the superficial. I'd based my perceptions on what seemed obvious from humankind's highways but which ultimately turned out to be totally wrong. I'd just not given Mississippi "ditches" a fair chance to reveal themselves as creeks with incredibly fine game fish stocks.

And there was another thing that struck me as I cranked up my truck and turned it around in the highway to head back home. Unlike most of my previous creek fishing experiences in other parts of the country, as well as abroad, this morning on the Mississippi creek I had not seen another angler or even a track from another human being. The only footprints I saw, other than my own, were those of wild critters. I saw no lost fishing tackle, absolutely none at all, on snags or overhanging limbs. It dawned on me that I had had the creek entirely to myself. That in itself was incredible. How could it be that these Mississippi treasures lay untapped? Were others like me, looking only from a distance and unwilling to probe to be sure that what they imagined was in fact reality?

Over the course of that summer I went to the other two streams near my home. On one of them I actually found rock outcroppings and waterfalls (in eastern Mississippi!). It also had more than a fair allotment of cottonmouths. Most behaved like gentlemen, holding their ground and letting me pass. However, one of the scoundrels actually chased me out of the creek, but just for a while . . . just long enough for me to cut a stick and engage (victoriously) in hand-to-hand combat with the beast. I was willing to share the creek, but it wasn't. Somebody had to win and that somebody was me. And the fishing was incredible. I caught several bass in it that weighed more than two pounds—that's *huge* for creek bass—and they were particularly feisty on my ultralight spinning tackle. On the other stream, I had to walk long distances between fishable pools, but when I got to the pools, the bass were stacked up in them and did everything they could to rip apart my lure (sometimes several fish trying to do it at the same time!) and then, when hooked they tried to tear the rod from my hands. One of the bass had a crooked back, and over the course of the next few years I caught that same bass several times.

One morning on this particular creek, as I was returning to my truck and approaching the pool that was just upstream from the bridge, I almost made a fatal mistake. It was Sunday and about 12:30 in the afternoon. People were heading home from church services for their fried chicken dinners. I'd played hookey. As people generally will, most looked out through their car windows and down at the creek as they drove over the bridge. (Ever wonder why so many car wrecks happen on bridges?) And there I stood, in front of God and everybody, thigh deep in the water, fishing rod in hand. Then, to make it even worse, in a moment of insanity, I did the unthinkable. I made a cast. I twitched the lure and in an instant was fast to a spotted bass that weighed over three pounds! (I actually weighed it.) And it was a jumper. It could not keep from trying to fly. Time and time again it surged and boiled and then left its watery realm. My little rod strained and I was sure that with the tension that the bass would soon break the light line. But it didn't.

It took forever for me to get that fish to hand. I'd hear a car coming down the highway, approaching the bridge, and I'd dip my rod down, releasing tension and doing the best that I could to have a dejected, forlorn, disappointed look about me as the car passed over the bridge and people gawked. From time to time, while doing this, I could see that bass cruising out there in the pool with my lure hanging from the corner of its mouth. Then, when the car was gone, I'd tighten up again and the bass, by then somewhat rested, would repeat its incredible performance. I was absolutely scared to death that somebody would see me with a bowed rod, or see that fish, or catch me with an involuntary grin on my face.

Digging as deeply as I could into my Deep South cultural heritage, I did the best that I could to remind myself, "It's best not to let on." By the time I had that fish in hand and was hiding (trembling) under the bridge, I was an emotional wreck. What in the world was that fish doing in that ditch pool by the bridge? And what on earth was I thinking when I make that final cast?!

So now, remembering how I was, sitting under that bridge, with bass in hand (and cars rolling by overhead) . . . as I pause a little and think about all this stuff that I've just written . . . it is dawning on me that I probably need to just go ahead and tear up the hard copies of this chapter, throw away the scraps of paper, purge all files, and send this entire piece into the forgotten realms of oblivion. But if by chance I fail to destroy this thing, and somehow in the future you happen to get your hands on a copy, just forget everything it says and keep driving over the bridges. There's nothing (but me) in those Mississippi "ditches."

Just One More Drop

Gold brushed the topmost branches of trees surrounding the small clearing in front of me. The hush of an early November evening settled on the landscape. Not a leaf stirred. From my deer stand, tucked in the shadows of a giant water oak, I could hear the faint rustling of brown thrashers as they worked the newly fallen leaves. Below me was a brush pile from cuttings I'd made two weeks earlier to open a shooting lane. A Carolina wren prowled the maze. A fox squirrel had been in the tree with me a few moments earlier, bold but cautious, trying to figure out what I was. Curiosity satisfied or perhaps growing bored, it had left me in peace and went on about its business until eventually disappearing from view. It would be dark in thirty minutes.

I'd been down in Jackson, Mississippi, earlier that day with my wife, watching our daughter Anna run in a cross-country meet for her high school. It had been a glorious day and a wonderful family outing, full of festivity, friends, and fellowship. After the meet, rather than taking the fastest route home, my wife and I decided to take the Natchez Trace Parkway. Anna would ride back in the bus with her teammates.

As we turned onto the parkway we entered a magical realm. Leaves were in full color and just beginning to fall, opening up the forest and allowing woods-rambling eyes to penetrate ever more deeply into the forest. It didn't take much imagination to envision leprechauns and fairies in some of the darker shadows. The creeks were low and clear. From time to time we'd see a fox squirrel scratching around and exploring on the roadside; then, seeing our car coming, it would turn and, in the slow, deliberate way of fox squirrels, move off toward the woods, dignity intact.

I mentioned to my wife that once we were home I thought I'd get on my tractor and work out on our farm for a while. I had some trails that needed mowing and a small wildlife food plot to disk. The farm is only six miles from our house and tucked back half a mile off of the main county road south of Starkville. It is my refuge, my sanctuary. An afternoon on my tractor is simply an excuse to be out there. The tractor is just one of my many sacraments . . . linking me with truths in another realm and with the rhythms of the earth. But by the time we pulled into our driveway I knew that I could not fill the afternoon or the evening with tractor noise. I needed to engage a different sacrament. It was a perfect afternoon for a deer hunt.

When I got out of the car I walked directly into my study and pulled out my bow and a practice broad-head arrow from their case. Then I went to my shed and wrestled the archery target from the dusty shelf where it had been stored since the previous deer season. In the months leading up to the deer season my work had precluded practice with the bow until that moment. I was anxious to see if I could still shoot. I was also concerned that I had not practiced and had not toned the muscles necessary to get that seventy-pound bow to full draw. I was in good physical shape from regular exercise, but different muscles are required for pulling a bow to full draw.

Setting up the target down by the shed, I walked back to my patio, pulled up a chair, took a seat, placed the arrow on the bow and pulled back. The distance to the target was twenty-five yards. I got to full draw without a problem. Steadying the bow sight on the target, I released the arrow and was pleased to see it slice into the center of the target. I shot twice more with the same results. That was all I needed in order to stroke my confidence.

It was 4:00 p.m. when I finished my target practice—time to make my move as a hunter. Sunset would be around 6:30 p.m. Twenty minutes later I'd taken a shower, changed into my hunting clothes, grabbed my gear, and was crawling into my pickup truck. It was 4:40 when I pulled up to the gate of my farm. I parked the truck and started walking quietly down the little dirt road that leads back to where I hunt deer on the place.

As I walked my heart started to swell. This would be my first day in the woods as a deer hunter this year, even though the archery season was over one month old. I could feel the hunter's spirit flow through me in full force. It was a wonderful feeling. The blue sky of late afternoon blended with the smoky smell of autumn. A redtail hawk soared over my pasture. Doves whistled up from the dusty corners of one of my wildlife food plots. It was good to be reconnecting.

I carefully and quietly worked my way to my deer stand. Although time was of the essence, I didn't hurry. I didn't want to start sweating and I didn't want to make too much noise. I also didn't want my scent anywhere in or around the clearing I'd be watching.

So I took the long route to the stand, along the opposite side of my farm, across a fence, and into a neighbor's pasture. I skirted my property line, far out into my neighbor's pasture, before making a sharp turn back to the south to come in on the backside of where my stand was positioned. Rather than a ten-minute walk directly to my stand, my circuitous route took me over twenty minutes. Even though it wasn't very hot, I was concerned about sweating, and the scent of sweat, and so had carried my light hunting jacket rather than wearing it. I didn't want to fill my stand with scent, even though the stand is nearly twelve feet up in the tree and there was no wind.

Once at the stand I quickly scaled the ladder and took position on the platform. I had an old plastic bucket up on the platform for a seat and had brought a boat cushion with me to make the seat a bit more comfortable. There would be only one planned movement from the time I sat down on that bucket until I left the stand at dark. In fifteen minutes, after I was sure that I had cooled down, I would stand, put on my jacket, lightweight gloves, and face mask, and then settle back down for the duration. I wasn't concerned about becoming chilled. I was more interested in the dark camouflage patterns on the jacket, the covering of my light-colored face and beard, and the fact that my light-colored hands would be the only thing moving in dark shadows if I were to draw on a deer. I needed something to darken those hands. But before I put on the jacket, mask, and gloves, I needed to be sure that I wasn't still hot.

That movement, putting on the jacket, mask, and gloves, had been nearly an hour ago, and now the world was becoming dusky and increasingly quiet. A pair of wood ducks whistled overhead and landed in a woodland pond about a hundred yards in front of me. A gray squirrel slipped through a tangle of vines and along the branch of a tree on the other side of the clearing. There were, at most, ten more minutes of shooting light. If this had been a gun hunt, I'd have had another twenty minutes of shooting light because of the light-gathering properties of a rifle's telescopic sight. But with a bow, there is no such sight. The sight of my bow is just a tiny metal bead on the end of a slender metal post. When I can't see the bead, I can't shoot.

Tucked back into the deepening shadows, completely still except for slow, rhythmic breathing and the movement of my eyes, I was for all practical purposes nonexistent in the forest. The evening that was gathering around me was beautiful beyond description. Then . . . a buck stepped out into the clearing.

At thirty yards he was just at the edge of my capabilities with the bow, but my confidence in the shot was strong and intact. Without hesitation he walked further out into the clearing, grazing on tender shoots of young wheat. My bow was already up and ready. He turned and gave me a perfect broadside shot. Carefully and deliberately I tightened my pull and started the draw. The target was perfect but . . . I could not get that bow to full draw! Sitting as I had been for nearly two hours, in the increasing chill of the November evening, my muscles had cooled and grown stiff, and I could *not* get that bow drawn. When I'd practiced earlier that afternoon, I was fresh from a two-hour drive and the afternoon had been relatively warm. I had not anticipated the effects of chilling on a tree stand. The situation was serious. Opportunity was fading fast.

The buck continued feeding and gave me another excellent target. Once again I tried and failed to get the bow to full draw. The buck ambled closer, to within twenty yards, still unaware of me. It was getting dark. Because of the darkness closing in, I told myself that I could risk a little extra movement. So, rather than drawing straight back on the bow string, I pointed the arrow up, locked my right arm and hand in position and pulled down with my left arm to get the bow into shooting position. That did it! I was at full draw! But . . . now it was so dark that I couldn't see the bead on the end of my sighting pin. The buck was clearly visible out in the middle of the clearing, but I couldn't tell where that bead was by looking through the peep sight attached to my bow string. So, with the bow still at full draw, I moved my head from side to side until I could see that bead. Once located, I slowly moved my eyes back and forth from bead to peep sight until I had that bead where I wanted it. Immediately the buck gave me another clear broadside target and I released the arrow.

I watched that beautiful arrow track perfectly to the target and disappear as it struck the deer. The buck whirled, dropped low to the ground and, within less than two seconds, it vanished into the darkness of the woods. There had been no sound except the whisper of the arrow in flight and the whisper of small branches as the deer entered the woods. Now, it was quiet beyond imagining. I listened carefully, hoping to hear the kicking or thrashing of a dying deer. But there was nothing. Nothing at all. No final bird song to mark the end of the day. No owl hoot or frog call to mark the beginning of night. No coyote howl to let me know that I was not the only hunter in the area. No late gray squirrel rustling the branches. No distant dog barking . . . nothing but quiet.

From where I sat, I mentally marked the spot in the clearing where the deer had been standing when I shot. I also carefully marked the spot where the deer had disappeared into the woods. Only then did I climb down from the stand and quietly, deliberately, go to the first spot. There was still a faint light in the sky. I looked all around. I could see no blood. Then, just beyond where I stood, I saw my arrow sticking up in the ground. I went to it, pulled it out of the ground and felt the stickiness of blood covering the shaft and vanes. With the arrow in hand, I went to the spot where I'd seen the deer go into the woods and hung my hat on a tree branch to mark the location. Now it was dark . . . absolutely . . . completely.

I walked back across my farm to my truck, put the bow in its case and the arrow on my dashboard, got a flashlight and a piece of cord, locked the truck, and walked back to my hat. With the flashlight I looked for blood. There was no blood, anywhere. Ducking through the hole in the brush and vines that the deer had passed through, and on into the woods, I continued looking for blood. Slowly, ever so slowly, flashlight working across every leaf and twig, I moved, one step at a time. Thirty minutes later I'd covered perhaps fifty feet. Still no blood. This concerned me but did not surprise me. At least half of the deer I'd shot with arrows during years past had not bled very much. Their trails had in some cases been extremely difficult to follow. But there had always been enough of a blood trail that I had been able to find them. The blades of a modern broad-head are so sharp that sometimes the skin of a deer simply closes back over the wound and there isn't much blood at all . . . on the outside. Inside the deer, however, it is a completely different situation.

Most deer shot well with an arrow, particularly if the arrow passes through the lungs, will only live from eight to ten seconds before they are on the ground. But a deer can move a considerable distance in eight to ten seconds. Deer are incredibly strong and fast. A deer that is *not* well shot can travel seemingly forever. I know this all too well also.

Finally, after an hour of searching, and at a distance of less than a hundred feet from the edge of the clearing, I found a tiny drop of blood on the edge of a leaf. This is what I needed. The line between point of entry into the woods and that first drop of blood gave me trajectory, showing me the direction of travel that the wounded deer had taken. I stopped right there and took the cord out of my jacket pocket. Carefully I wrapped the cord around my flashlight and tied the light onto a branch. Then I punched the button on the light, adjusting the beam to the dimmest light possible, and walked out of the woods. I needed that light to shine for a long time. The dim beam would be enough for me to find the light in the dark woods later that evening. I was going home . . . for more batteries, for flagging tape, and for a quick supper.

Nearly two hours later I was back at my farm gate parking my truck. As I walked across my pasture and back to the corner of my farm where I'd shot the deer, I saw shadowy movements as other deer moved in front of me. It was very dark. There would be no moon until much later that night. But the starlight was magnificent. And the stars themselves hung as jewels in the black sky.

Sometimes stars seem all to be in one level, without giving any sense of depth to the sky, but this night there was something about them that emphasized the infinite space of the universe . . . layer after layer . . . on and on and on. Looking at them, I shivered, but the chill that coursed through me did not come from the autumn air. It is a feeling that comes to me when I sense that God is very near . . . and that I am doing the right thing. With that chill I was reminded of my small place in creation, both in terms of place and time. I was reminded also of my identity, an identity that through the years has pulled me ever deeper into the realms of the wild, as a hunter in pursuit of the hunted. And in that regard, out there, somewhere in the dark, was the deer that I'd shot. The deer was probably dead. I needed to find it. Little did I know what lay before me. Little did I know the full extent of what that chill I'd felt really meant.

As I neared the clearing where I'd shot the deer, I could see the faint glow of my flashlight back in the woods. After crossing the clearing and working my way back through the woods to the light, I prepared to resume tracking. From my jacket pocket I pulled out a package of fresh batteries for the flashlight and a roll of flagging tape that had reflector strips. Long ago I'd learned that without those reflector strips even the brightest colored tape was tough to see in thick woods during the night. I replaced the battery in the flashlight, cranked up the brightness, tied a strip of tape to the branch that had held the light, and started the search for the next drop of blood.

It took nearly thirty minutes to find that next drop. It was actually more of a smear on the side of a tiny branch. I tied another strip of tape and moved forward. The next drop came quickly, within ten feet. I tied a strip and proceeded. Then another twenty minutes passed before I found a new drop . . . nearly fifty feet from the last one.

Sometimes it takes awhile for the body cavity of a deer to fill up with blood to the extent that it starts exiting wounds. This tends to be the case if wounds are high on the chest. But now I was starting to get concerned. There should have been a better blood trail by now, if there was going to be one. I pushed on, slowly, looking at every leaf on the ground, every twig and branch in the undergrowth. This deer had moved into some of the thickest growth in that part of the woods—not an unusual move for a wounded deer, but one that makes tracking tremendously challenging. The deer obviously had been thinking about its escape and not just plunging blindly into cover.

Archery tends to be a quiet, efficient, almost painless way to kill deer. And it requires that the deer be very close. Deer shot with arrows are not shocked the way that they are when shot with a gun. After being shot they are still thinking clearly . . . for a while. The razor-sharp arrow stings as it passes through them, but sometimes deer even continue feeding after being shot by an arrow. After a few moments, the shot deer gets dizzy from loss of blood and goes down. In my experience, deer shot with arrows on average actually tend to go down quicker than those shot with a gun. Thus is the magic of bow hunting and its beauty, which combine into a mixture that fills a hunter's soul at times almost to the bursting point. It certainly fills mine.

One hour, seventy-five feet, and two AA flashlight batteries later there still was no heavy blood trail. My world shrank to the diameter of a tiny circle of light. My focus intensified. The drops that I did find were sporadic, very small, and widely spaced. Then, about thirty feet in front of me, I saw the edge of a steep bluff. At the bottom of the bluff was a shallow creek. From past experience tracking wounded deer through these woods, I knew that there were only a few ways down that bluff to the creek. On the other side was another steep bluff, again with only a few ways up. Once on top of the other side I also knew that the woods changed character dramatically. It became more jungle than forest, with thick vines and underbrush and ground covered by pine needles rather than hardwood leaves. Wounded deer shot on my place almost always try to make it to that jungle. Blood would be even more difficult to find in those needles.

The blood trail went almost to the edge of the bluff and then it stopped. There was no blood to the left or to the right for fifty feet. I circled, thinking that perhaps the buck would backtrack, but in my heart I knew that a wounded deer rarely, if ever, does this. They'll do it when they are being chased by dogs or by hunters before a shot, but if wounded, they move forward until they are almost at their end. Then and only then do they become erratic.

Finding no more blood anywhere, I decided to go down into the creek and look upstream and downstream. There might be blood on the rocks alongside the creek or perhaps a red glint in some tiny pocket of water. There might even be a fresh track with little pieces of dirt still crumbling inside of it. I was looking for anything . . . anything at all.

I traveled a hundred yards downstream, scouring both banks, looking for sign. Then I reversed direction, went back to my entry point where I'd come down the slope and traveled a hundred yards upstream, looking for sign. There was nothing, nothing at all. The deer had vanished.

I looked at my watch. It was nearing midnight. The moon rose. I stopped where I was and just stood still . . . very, very, still . . . out there in the middle of the creek, in the dark, in the chill, thinking, reaching deeply into my reserves as a hunter, drawing on years of experience as a hunter with many deer to his credit, and drawing on something that was more within a spiritual realm to help me put this hunt, this tracking into some sort of perspective. I needed a new framework. I needed a new direction. Owls were calling. I heard a distant coyote. I'd shot that deer over five hours ago. Where was it? *Where was it?!*

I decided that I needed to return to my discipline, go back to the last drop of blood I'd marked with reflector tape up on top of the bluff and keep on working, slowly, deliberately, in a world defined by quiet reflection, focused thought, determination, and a tiny circle of light. It is not my habit to pray for success as a hunter but rather to give prayers of thanksgiving when there has been a successful hunt. But I broke from this tradition and prayed that I would have the skill, the resourcefulness, and, if possible, divine help in finding just one more new drop of blood. That's all I wanted. It had been over an hour since I'd seen a new drop. Just one more new drop . . . please.

Rather than climbing back up the bluff the way I'd come down it, I decided for some reason to claw my way up a narrow ravine. It was choked by fallen tree branches and roots and was only about four feet wide at its widest point. It went almost straight up, but the branches and vines gave me the hand and foot holds I needed . . . more like going up a ladder than anything else. I was concerned as I climbed that I'd slip and either fall or get wedged somehow and break an ankle or leg. So I moved slowly, testing each hold, until finally I was able to put my hand on the top of the bluff. I grabbed a small sapling that grew on that edge and with my other hand shined my light on the ground in front of me. There, within inches of my face, level with my eyes, was a drop of blood. My heart leaped. My prayer had been answered. I quickly said another prayer of thanksgiving. That drop was at least a hundred yards from where I'd marked the last drop I'd found before going down into the creek. The only way possible to see that new drop was from the vantage point of a person climbing up that ravine and whose face was inches off the ground.

Although I couldn't imagine a deer coming down that limb- and root-choked little ravine I'd just scaled, that's exactly what that wounded deer had done. It had wanted to cross that creek and get to the jungle on the other side, and it had wanted to do it quickly. The little ravine, dangerous though it was for a deer to traverse, was the quickest way down.

I climbed back down the ravine and into the creek bed and stood there, thinking. It wasn't a matter of tracking anymore. I had to get out of that mindset. I had to transition. I had to think like a deer . . . a wounded deer . . . a weakening deer. The deer had come down a very rough entrance into the creek's channel. It had probably stumbled, even if only a little, and, in regaining its footing, had probably left a track somewhere on the side of the creek. I went to the base of the little ravine and looked very hard. There was a fresh deer track imprinted in small shale gravel on the edge of the water, but no blood. I crossed the creek and looked for another track. There was no track. The deer may have come down here but it did not cross the creek. There were also no tracks alongside the creek. It had traveled in the center of the creek, in the water. There was clear water in the creek and it flowed across a solid sheet of shale. It was very shallow, perhaps three or four inches deep at most. There would be nothing to guide me. I looked at my watch. It was now 12:30 a.m. I committed myself anew to the task, put a fresh battery in my flashlight, and developed a strategy.

That deer would have been looking for a gradual slope in order to get up the opposite bank and into the jungle on the other side. It would not have tried to go up a steep bank. The deer very likely had been too weak to do that. But *I* could climb that bluff, and I did. I knew that there was no gentle slope along the bluffs going downstream, but I seemed to recall such a slope upstream. So that was the direction I intended to travel.

I crossed the creek, climbed the opposite bank, and walked the edge of the bluff, slowly moving upstream, shining my light down from the edge, looking for gentle swales or shelves that would invite a wounded deer to attempt an assent. Ten minutes later my light caught the glint of something shining in the dark. I stopped, focused the light to a tighter beam, and there in front of me, eyes shining, lay my deer . . . a beautiful four-point buck, stretched out on a small shelf of ground just above the creek channel, nestled in a carpet of crushed ferns.

I carefully rappelled down the bluff using a grapevine to assist me and approached the buck. I looked at its side and saw the place where the arrow had entered. A perfect shot. I grabbed one front leg and one hind leg and rolled him over so that I could look at the other side. He was stiff and cold. He had been dead for hours and had already cooled. I expected to see blood on the deer's other side and on the ground, but there was hardly any at all. I looked at the wound where the arrow had exited the deer. Just like the entry wound, it was perfectly placed but there just wasn't any blood.

I field dressed the buck where it lay and found the blood. It was all trapped inside the deer. By bleeding out (albeit internally) and then chilling so quickly on this cool November night, this deer would be in excellent shape as venison for my family. I could not have asked for anything better. I whispered a second prayer, one of thanksgiving for this buck, and also a prayer for strength and stamina to get that buck across the creek, up the bluff via the ravine, through the woods, and to my pasture where I could get it loaded into my truck. It was going to be tough. I knew that I could do it, but at age fifty-eight I also knew that I would have to take my time and be very careful. If I had an accident, it would be very hard for anyone to find me this far back in the woods.

I remember watching the creek wash blood from the deer's body cavity as I sloshed along down in the channel, holding onto its antlers, dragging the deer in the clear water behind me. I remember going vertical with that buck, one root or branch step at a time up the ravine, finally wrapping one arm around the sapling at the top of the ravine and hoisting that buck somehow with one arm up and over the lip of the ravine. I don't know where such strength comes from, but I've experienced it on numerous occasions on other hunts or when engaged in similar challenging outdoor situations. When it is needed, it is there. Then there was the drag across leaves and over logs and through vines to and beyond the barbed-wire fence near the clearing where the buck had been shot, and, leaving the buck in the clearing, the quiet walk across my farm back to the truck parked at the gate, with stars and the moon so bright I could see my shadow on the pasture. I took a deep breath at the beauty of it all . . . all that was around me and all that was in me.

An hour and a half after starting the trek from where I'd found and field dressed the buck on the slope beside the creek, I was locking the gate to my farm. Then as I pulled away from the gate in my truck there was the crunching of gravel on the road heading home. Starlight and moonlight bathed the countryside. Satisfaction bathed my heart.

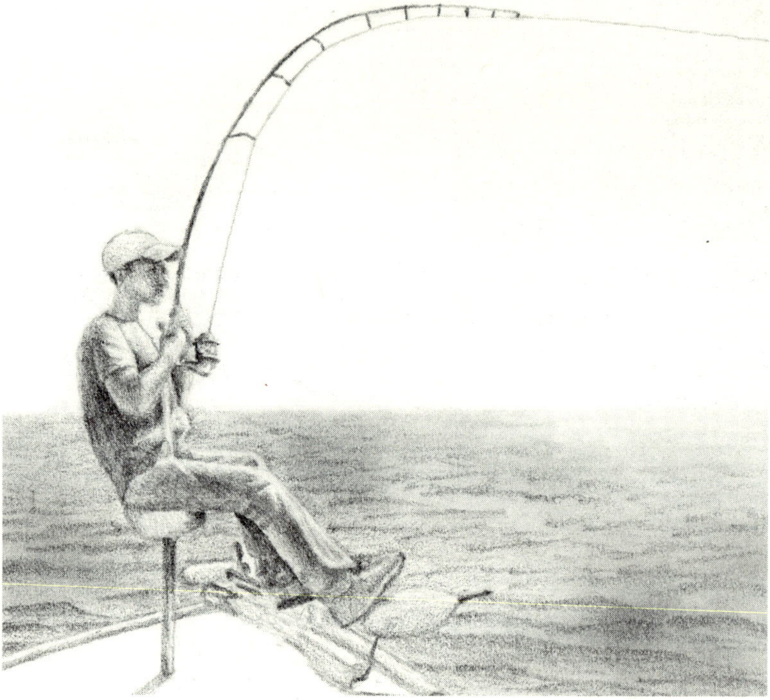

It Takes a Friend

I've avoided turkey hunting for good reason. I went once, had a turkey strutting right in front of me at fifteen feet, and simply watched that wonderful bird until it got tired of showing off and simply drifted away. It never dawned on me to raise my shotgun and shoot the thing. I realized right then and there, on my first turkey hunt, that I had to stop turkey hunting *immediately* or risk losing wife, family, home, and job. I knew that if I started turkey hunting before retirement, before my kids were grown, before my house was paid for, I'd be living alone in some shack or junky house trailer under scraggly pines, with a beat-up pickup truck on a clean-swept dirt front yard, perhaps with a couple of mutt dogs under the porch, an old boat on a rusty trailer, and two or three well-worn shotguns.

I was then and continue to be a turkey-hunting junkie. It is a physiological condition, perhaps genetic in origin. My hunting companions, most of whom are turkey hunters, completely understand and have supported me, giving me much needed encouragement, as I've fought to maintain discipline. From time to time, however, when the woods are just starting to awaken in spring, when soft breezes from the south temper the northwest winds and cardinals are starting to sing just before sunrise, I'll slip my leash, grab my shotgun, owl hooter, and turkey call, and go out to my farm "just to listen." I have a little drove of turkeys out there that tease me in my affliction. I move through the predawn shadows, trembling, fighting for self-control, and, after a gobble or two and perhaps a cluck or a purr from my box call, somehow find the strength to turn and walk back to my truck as the turkeys answer my calling.

I had been warned by many about this disease before that first turkey hunt. And I know that my teaser hunts on the farm are extremely dangerous. Give an alcoholic but a single drop and he's back in the gutter again. But . . . as I write this, there are only three years left, more or less, until I release myself from bondage and start chasing those birds. I'll be so close to retirement by then that it won't really matter at work, and my kids will all be pretty much on their semi-independent runways and won't need (or want) me around very much. And as for my wife . . . well . . . she gave up on me years ago when she found out that I would duck hunt every morning during the season (whether there were any ducks or not), deer hunt almost every evening from October through January, and, during the summer, consistently be late for church because I would be fly-fishing for bluegill on my pond.

Now she and the kids just keep talking about whatever, or doing whatever, when I bust through the door to the kitchen, covered with mud, blood, or sometimes both, and announce that I've got a fine buck out in the truck or that the ducks worked perfectly to decoys, and boy was I on them, or that the bluegill were in a feeding fit. Typically, however, only the dogs seem interested in what I have to say or show, and so I take them out to the carport for a sniff.

Little does my family know that the afflictions of duck hunting and deer hunting and fly-fishing for bluegill are nothing compared to those of turkey hunting. I don't talk about it. Some things are best just left alone until they can no longer be avoided. There will be plenty of time to talk turkey. And I'm so proud of myself for my ability to recognize danger before disaster and to maintain (somewhat) my discipline.

Pride, however, sets a man up for disaster. Having avoided turkey hunting, I thought I was somehow beyond reach of serious vice and that nothing less than civil war or nuclear holocaust had real potential to rock my boat. The little woman, the children, the fine house on the corner, situated in a respectable neighborhood, with a big lawn to mow twice a week, my job at the university, my status within my profession, and my place in the community . . . all seemed safe and secure. Yes siree . . . the MAN was in control.

Everybody has secrets. One of mine is that I'd never learned how to fish in salt water. I'd read about it. I'd dreamed about it. I'd watched shows about it. I was around people who did it. But nobody ever introduced me to it. Everybody thought I was in the game, but I wasn't. I had absolutely no idea where to start or how to start. It's like covering up illiteracy. A man can fake it for a very long time, and I did.

I didn't grow up around the ocean. My world was rivers, lakes, swamps, and ponds. When I was a Peace Corps volunteer I messed around on tropical beaches and an island or two, went sailing in the South Seas, and did some snorkeling on coral reefs, but I never actually *fished* in the ocean. I didn't know how, and overseas nobody seemed to fish for fun. It was all about nets and traps and either selling or eating fish. In fact, it wasn't until years later, when I was thirty years old and in graduate school studying fisheries, that I actually got on an honest to gosh, "sho-nuf," ocean-going fishing boat, a research ship with the National Marine Fisheries Service. I was out on the big blue water for a couple of weeks and dragged nets all over the bottom of the Gulf of Mexico. It was a great experience.

Over the years I maintained my connection with that old ship, the *Oregon II*, and regularly went to sea onboard her with my students. I learned about the marine fish and the fisheries and even taught courses in marine fisheries at the university. But it was all about commercial and subsistence fisheries, fisheries policy, and administration. Understanding population dynamics, marine ecology, and ocean politics does little to help a man learn how to fish in the sea. I knew nothing about recreational angling in marine environments. Although I hungered for saltwater fishing, *my* fishing continued to be in freshwater.

Twenty years passed . . . nearly a full career in fisheries . . . and I found myself elected as an officer in the Mississippi Wildlife Federation, still without any significant saltwater angling experience. There were coastal issues to tend to on behalf of the organization, and I continued to address then professionally from environmental, conservation, socioeconomic, and political perspectives. Everybody assumed that I also fished salt water, until one day I confided in a fellow officer, Linwood Grierson, who worked as a banker for Merchant and Marine Bank down in Pascagoula, Mississippi. Soon thereafter Hurricane Katrina hit the Mississippi Gulf Coast and nothing else mattered.

In the wake of the hurricane I applied for and was granted a sabbatical from the university to help restore coastal fisheries. Simultaneously, and in addition to my work with the Mississippi Wildlife Federation, I headed up the American Fisheries Society's hurricane relief program. For a two-year period I worked with state and federal fisheries agencies, established research as well as restoration programs, coordinated relief efforts for coastal fisheries professionals and their institutions, and continually integrated the voice of the Mississippi Wildlife Federation and the American Fisheries Society into the mix through presentations, seminars, workshops, and courses.

It would be an understatement to say that Linwood Grierson and I connected during this period of trial. I lost count of my trips and days to and on the coast, but he was ever present—just a phone call or a few minutes away, and standing at ready to make stuff happen. We spent many an evening in his home, many a lunch at local restaurants, and many a civic club meeting dealing with the hurricane response and relief issues at hand. I was a "regular" at the motel in Moss Point, Mississippi, where I stayed. The receptionists always kept a room available for me, and typically it was the same room. I learned to get around on the coast . . . what was left of it anyway . . . and watched with amazement its resurrection in the months following the hurricane. Through it all Linwood Grierson never forgot my secret, and as far as I know, he never revealed it to anyone. Then, as my sabbatical assignments ended and my term of office with the Mississippi Wildlife Federation wound down, Linwood said, "Let's go fishing."

Now getting an invitation to go fishing with Linwood Grierson is sort of like Hank Arron inviting you to a little batting practice down at the park, or Jack O'Conner asking if you'd like to go out to the range and shoot some "real" rifles, or Ernest Hemmingway asking you to join him for dinner to go over the manuscript of a new story. Linwood is *the* master light-tackle saltwater fisherman in the Pascagoula River estuary and bays and along the coast.

"Meet me at my house at 2:00 p.m. and we'll fish the low tide. But I have to quit fishing around 6:00 p.m. in order to make it to

Wednesday evening services at my church. Bring your bass fishing tackle. That's all you'll need."

As we backed the boat down the public ramp near city hall in Moss Point, I looked around me at a world that absolutely captured me, heart and soul. I loved the smell of the marsh. The dark water lapped gently at the seawall and pilings near the ramp. There was a glow on everything from the late afternoon sun. The air was so thick and salty that sweat just crusted up on my skin in a sort of paste. Across from the ramp was a marina where various boats were securely moored. Next to it was a bait shop specializing in shrimp (live or frozen) and "bull minnows." Linwood bought a couple of bags of ice and threw them into a large cooler he had in the boat.

As I stood there soaking it all in while helping Linwood launch his boat, I felt something come to life inside of me. It wasn't something I'd ever felt before . . . or so I thought at the time. I really wasn't too concerned about it either. It felt so good, so right, being there with my friend, going fishing . . . *just going fishing*. He said the tide was right and that the fishing should be good. I was completely unaware of the danger unfolding around me.

The new energy within me continued to swell as we cast off and cruised around to the end of a little spit of an island. In the distance I could see a shipyard and a new ship, the *R. V. Pisces*, being built. I knew about this ship. It was destined for the National Marine Fisheries Service fleet. I also knew that in all likelihood I'd someday sail on it, dragging nets, setting longlines, collecting data for fisheries assessments. Looking back at where we'd launched, I could see the marina, the bridge across the estuary, and a few buildings—an old fish processing plant, a few homes back among the live oaks beyond the marsh grass—and emerging mud flats as the tide continued to fall.

At the end of the island the water was very shallow and there were old pieces of wood, hard crusted with marine life, that we had to maneuver around. It took us a few minutes to break free of the shallow obstacle-ridden area. Then, on the backside of the little island, the water deepened. In fact we were in a little lagoon that was about a hundred yards wide at the most and was, maybe, a shade more than half a mile long. The water was absolutely like smooth glass on top. Whatever slight ripple may have been outside the lagoon, the surrounding barriers stopped. The tide now had fallen to a point where there was a lot of exposed mud back in pockets, and the water was perhaps a foot or two deep along the edge of the marsh grass. Shorebirds worked the mud and shallow water. A few gulls cruised high overhead. There was an awesome stillness out there. We spoke quietly but mostly just let the stillness sink in and stroke our hearts. The reflections on the water were surreal . . . with only the slightest distortion . . . just enough to let you know where water ended and land began. An osprey settled on an old snag. Dimples emerged from the water.

Linwood suggested a small gray top-water lure and I tied one on. Then I began to cast. Linwood corrected me. I was confused. But he said to wait until we saw a fish. *Saw a fish?* I followed his instructions, quit fishing, and just waited. I wasn't sure what was going on. Then he said, "There . . . there's a redfish right over next to those snags, working that little pocket of water."

I looked and saw a slight swirl in the water, then the tip of a fin. That was all I needed and I cast.

"No!" Linwood quietly said . . . but it was too late. The lure landed in front of the fish. I twitched the lure and the world exploded. The redfish made a quick run, wrapped the line around one of the snags, and immediately broke off and escaped.

"You've got to wait, Don, . . . wait until you have some clear water ahead of the fish and a better chance of getting the fish out here where its deep, where you can fight him."

It was a hard lesson. I'd felt something incredibly powerful as that rod had arched . . . something powerful on the end of my line and something equally as powerful in my soul. I really didn't know how big that fish had been, but Linwood said that it might have gone six to eight pounds. Six to eight pounds?! I'd caught other fish that size before and none of them had been *that* strong. To me, the fish had pulled like something over twenty pounds.

We slowly cruised the shoreline and then Linwood pointed out another dimple in the water. We were in business again.

Quietly, just like stalking a gray squirrel on a still morning in the woods, we slipped closer and closer to the fish. Linwood cautioned that I needed to be very sure of my cast because I'd probably only get one chance. A botched cast would probably spook the fish. So I waited as long as I could stand it. I was afraid that the fish would see the boat and spook. Then Linwood said, "Now," and I cast.

The little lure plopped into the water about thirty inches in front of the fish. I just let it sit there. I could see a slight ripple that told me the fish was still there.

"Twitch it, Don."

I did and the fish ripped into my lure.

This time there was no snag for the fish to break off on. It tore off into deep water, stripping line from my reel. I wondered if it would ever stop. Linwood was working the boat, backing it out carefully to the deep water with the fish.

"How's your drag? Is it set right?"

"I think so, Linwood. He's still ripping out line, but everything seems to be holding fine."

Finally, the fish slowed, then stopped. I tried to work in a little line. The fish felt the pressure and took off again, but this time the run wasn't quite as long. I tried again to gain some line, and this time I could feel the fish yielding. Slowly, rod bent, a heavy weight throbbing and pulling against me, I brought the fish toward the boat. I got it about halfway to me and it took off again, stripping off the line I'd gained. I started the process all over again, glanced over to Linwood, and saw him just sitting there in his boat seat, a big grin all over his face.

Gain a little, lose a little; with each cycle the fish came just a little closer to the boat. I simply could not imagine a fish with such power and endurance, but this thing on the end of my line was absolutely for real. Finally, I saw the fish . . . and it saw me and took off again! It took another five or six minutes to work it back to the boat. It was only then that I saw Linwood reach for his landing net. I did the best I could to steer the fish toward the net, but just at the critical moment, it plunged away into the deep again and I had to work it some more. That, however, was its last real surge; and this time, when I steered the fish toward the net, Linwood was able to reach out and snatch that gorgeous fish from the water.

I had NEVER had such a fish on my line. I'd caught bigger fish, including salmon in Alaska, but I'd never had anything that strong to deal with. And I was amazed at its size.

"How big, Linwood?"

"Oh, about six pounds," and he handed me a cold Corona beer from his cooler. "Congratulations partner . . . that's a fine redfish."

"It's my first, Linwood."

"I know." And he just sat there grinning at me as I tried to recover. The beer helped.

"OK, let's go find another one."

Ten minutes later I was fast to redfish number two. Rather than striking hard when the fish had hit the lure, I followed Linwood's advice: "Strike by feel, not by sight. When you *feel* the fish on the line, *then* set the hook."

As a bass fisherman, this was hard advice to follow, but I managed to do it and now was in business again, with a fine redfish determined to empty my reel's spool of line. But, just as had happened with the first fish, it eventually stopped, and the back and forth tug-of-war started. It seemed like an eternity before Linwood was able to scoop up the fish with his net, but he said it had only been about ten minutes, somewhat shorter than the time it had taken me to land the first one.

The tide was really going out by this time, and the sun's low angle turned the entire world around us golden. Small crabs scrambled across the exposed mud. A rail poked around in the grass and occasionally darted across an open spot. The sky and estuary were huge all around me and yet I was in a small world, focused hard on tasks at hand in a small lagoon, trying to see if I could spot another fish.

"Don, I think you're ready for a *real* redfish now. I've been watching a good one just down the shore. Let's go get him."

At first I didn't see the fish, but then I saw a bronzed-back monster crawl up into ten-inch deep water, swirl slightly, and continue cruising along the shoreline, occasionally in water so shallow that I couldn't imagine it could be swimming. It seemed to me that it was crawling like a lizard in those shallow spots.

We slowly approached the fish. I cast behind the boat once just to be sure I had the right feel for the cast to the fish. Then I sat very still, ready to cast at Linwood's command. Ahead of the fish was a side pocket of water about the size of a dining room table.

"Now," whispered Linwood.

And I cast into that pocket of water.

The redfish approached the edge of the pocket and I slowly pulled the lure out in front of it, careful not to jerk or make it sputter or spin. The redfish stopped about eight inches from the lure. I gave the lure a twitch that caused one of its propellers to buzz just a bit, and the world exploded—the monster came halfway out of the water with my little lure in the corner of its mouth. When it came back down I felt the weight of the fish and "struck on feel"—and that fish struck back, nearly ripping the spinning rod from my arms. Then came the fish's first hard run and a tap on my shoulder from Linwood.

I turned around and he had another cold beer extended to me.

"Take your time. You've got him, and he's a dandy."

I held the beer in one hand and the rod in the other as the redfish surged out into deep water and then headed down to the end of the lagoon. I had plenty of line, and Linwood assured me that as long as we stayed here in deep water we'd be fine. And we were.

I played that wonderful fish, with my wonderful friend—grinning and occasionally laughing—right there in the boat with me, coaching and encouraging me as I wrestled with the monster in the deep. In and out, run after run, once a glimpse of the fish, then it was off again. The beer was finished but the fish was not. For over fifteen minutes I fought that red rascal out there in that dark water, with my soul about as close to euphoria as it had ever been. The osprey took off from its perch. The sun sank to the water's surface below and beyond the bridge over the river. The fish bore deeply, then ran again and again and again. I just held on and cranked when I could. Then, magically, it came alongside the boat, and with one swift lunge, Linwood had it in the net.

He placed the fish, still in the net, on the bottom of the boat. The fish shimmered in the late evening light. I was speechless. I could not take my eyes off of it.

"He'll go better than ten pounds, Don, maybe even as much as eleven or twelve. That's a good fish, Don, . . . a very fine fish."

All I could do was just sit there, thoughts swirling, heart pounding . . . as the world spun around me and that fish and my friend filled my heart.

It was then that terror struck. Out there on the water, in that boat, with a golden sunset setting the world on fire, the smells and sounds of the estuary flooding my senses, and that big redfish stretched out in front of me, visions of pending disaster suddenly, and without warning, engulfed me. I struggled—but just a little—to defend myself. Then I surrendered, absolutely and completely.

The MAN who had for many years deftly avoided catastrophe in the clutches of turkey hunting now realized that he'd been blindsided by redfish fishing. Whether intentional or not, the deed had been done and now there was no turning back. My mind was awash with visions of a new boat, a new and stronger truck to tow it, and life in a lonely, weatherboard shack on some tidal creek or bay. The prospects of family and career neglect that would have resulted from turkey hunting, and which had been held successfully at bay for decades, now were rearing their ugly heads from salt water. The seeds of dark and devious strategy were already sprouting as I sat there in the boat . . . the smooth "weasel words" needed to justify long days, extra days, early departures from home and the university, and late returns in order to get done *what needed to get done* (specifics undefined) down on the coast. The sirens were calling my name. And I was being lured to the treacherous shoals.

I looked at Linwood, seeking a helping hand from him as I fought for balance on the edge of the precipice, seeking some words of wisdom from the sage of the estuary, or perhaps a sign of hope . . . and all I got, as he cranked the outboard motor on the boat and headed back to the launching ramp, was one more grin and another cold beer.

A Treatment for Woods Rambling Syndrome

WHY DO WE FIDGET ON DEER STANDS ON AFTERNOONS SO STILL you can hear mice rustling in the leaves? Why, after setting out decoys, do we slosh our waders and hip boots in the water . . . even before wood ducks start flying? What is it that compels us to take the long way back to the truck after a hunt? What was it, back when Mr. Bob reigned as the Prince, that caused us to chase raw-boned pointers, classy setters, and pumped-up Brittany spaniels for hours on end across the treasures of a Deep South landscape? Why do we explore creeks and hollows and traverse ridges as sunsets fill the world with shadows and gold and evening chill settles on the land, knowing that we'll be using starlight to find our way home?

It isn't because we lack patience. It fact, as hunters, we are masters at patience. We take every opportunity to practice it. During sermons, seminars, meetings, lectures, most high school plays, and all operas, we focus on whoever is making the delivery and, with incredible discipline, suddenly see the individual transformed into nobility . . . the glint off glasses becoming that of sunlight on antlers, the drift from podium or pulpit or across a stage becoming the strut of a gobbler. With eyes focused (albeit perhaps somewhat glazed over) and breathing stilled and rhythmic (until the spouse beside us punches us in the side), we demonstrate patience and persistence of the highest order.

The truth of the matter is that most of us hunters are afflicted with woods rambling syndrome. It is treatable but incurable. It is not something that can be addressed simply by searching for arrowheads and fossils, bird watching, identifying wildflowers, rolling logs for salamanders, amusing yourself shaking muscadine vines, checking to see how deep a creek is while wearing knee boots, or standing on one leg trying to unhook a strand of barbed wire from the crotch of your hunting britches. These activities are helpful and certainly can be part of the prescription, but to address the syndrome head on you have to pick up your gun and go squirrel hunting. I repeat: *Go squirrel hunting.*

You are a hunter . . . so *hunt*. Go looking for the critter you're after. Don't just bushwhack it by waiting for it from back in the shadows of some hidey-hole. Sneak up on Mr. Bushytail (if you can), make a good shot (awesome responsibility), and feel good about responding to a call of the wild deep inside of you that is primeval in origin. Remember . . . you are a predator. When you shoot a squirrel, you've just done what your genes have been directing you and your predecessors to do over the tumbling generations of humankind. You have two eyes on the front of your face that give you the binocular vision characteristic of all visually oriented predators. You can focus on your prey (remember, you practiced doing this in church, in school, and at the opera). The fact that what you've just shot weighs less than a couple of pounds is immaterial. You are a successful *hunter* (not bushwhacker). And by *hunting*, you are treating your severe case of woods rambling syndrome, and I must say that you've just done it in grand style. It is OK to feel a little smug about doing this, but don't linger long in self-congratulation. Pick up your squirrel, put it in the sack, take a deep breath, adjust your hat, check the safety on your gun one more time, and step on out into the wild world around you.

Notice that I said "step out" into the world around you. I mean that. Take one step, then stop. That's absolutely essential to regaining your hunter's perspective. Take a couple of deep breaths. Look around you at the way the sun is filtering down through the trees. Watch that woodpecker working over the dead snag out ahead of you. Reach over to the big oak next to you and put your hand on the trunk. Amazing things, these big trees . . . these things that make the woods what it is. Get right under it and look straight up into the sky through its branches. Rub your hand across the bark, take another deep breath, reach back and feel the lump of squirrel in your sack or game pocket. Now take step number two and proceed with treating your case of woods rambling syndrome.

A word of warning is in order here. About this time, usually step number two, sometimes step number three, a 200-class whitetail buck will usually jump up in front of you and head off in the direction of the deer stand that you obviously are not sitting in. Do not kick yourself in the butt. You are a sick person engaged in treating your syndrome. If you rush back to your truck for bow or deer rifle at this point, your affliction will only intensify. (Now be honest . . . your bow or deer rifle *is* in the truck, isn't it? That's OK, I understand.) Get control of yourself. Hold steady to the course. The storm within you will pass. Take two more steps and calm down. Checking the safety on your gun once more at this point will help you regain focus. It is probably off because you instinctively brought the gun up when the buck came up in front of you. It is not your fault. But check that safety.

Look out ahead of you and proceed with rambling. Pay attention to that little rustling out ahead. Was it a puff of wind or something else? There it is again . . . a gray ghost working the tippy-top branches of a water oak at forty yards. And there is no direct way to close the distance. The spacing between trees is just too far. With the possible exception of a gobbler, there's nothing in the woods with sharper eyes than a gray squirrel. Put that squirrel eighty feet up in a tree and it is darn near impossible to avoid detection during a stalk—but you are going to try.

Sticking to the shadows, moving like a panther, one careful step at a time, no fast movements, it takes you over twenty minutes to close the gap. Something swells inside of you (no, it is not a heart attack). You feel something so right. You're in tune with your surroundings, absolutely. The gun in you hands is an extension of yourself. You've resurrected something you only now realize that you came close to losing. It's all coming together again. During these moments there is absolutely nothing more important than that squirrel still out in those tippy-top branches cutting acorns. You take a deep breath, then another. You are twelve years old again. The earth smells send you back across the years. You haven't been this way for a very long time. Slowly, you raise your gun and, using the tree beside of you, you settle the sight on the squirrel. But the rascal will not hold still (gray squirrels rarely do). You wait, gun ready for the split second of pause that will come, but you don't know when. Then it happens, and without hesitation, almost without thinking, you squeeze off the shot.

The gray squirrel is a tough critter. But it is hit and hit hard. For a moment it grips the branch it is on. Then it turns loose. Down it comes, an eighty-foot free fall through space that etches itself in your memory. With a thump it hits the ground, its tail-twisting leading you to the spot that you've riveted your eyes on. Just like when shooting doves, you know that you absolutely must keep your eye on the spot where it fell or risk losing it. Dead gray squirrels, unlike most dead fox squirrels, can simply disappear otherwise. Maybe it is my fifty-seven-year-old eyes, but I don't think so. Gray squirrels are without a doubt perfect woods animals. Even when dead on the ground, they are made to stay in the woods. When you get one with a good shot after a careful stalk, the *hunter* in you is approaching perfection in treating your woods rambling syndrome.

The gun that you use for squirrel hunting depends on two things: the gun that you have and the place where you hunt. I like to use a scope-sighted .22 rifle when I hunt places where there are few if any houses or highways within a mile. It is getting harder and harder to find places like this. But, as in all hunting, safety is absolutely the number one consideration. When the safety requirements for hunting with a .22 rifle cannot be met, I hunt with a shotgun. To *not* hunt squirrels is not an option. With a shotgun I still am rambling the woods, connecting with the earth, the day, and myself, and I still have to stalk the squirrels. Squirrels are easier to hit but harder to kill with a shotgun. With a shotgun, you'll generally have more crippled squirrels that you will have to run down and dispatch. As crude as it sounds, I've found that the best way to dispatch a squirrel is to grab it by the tail and swing it hard against the trunk of a tree. *Don't use the butt of your gunstock.*

Your gun could discharge and then there could be tragedy. And remember . . . a squirrel can (and will) bite, and bite hard.

There have been days when all of the magic was in the woods with me. I've hunted well. I've shot well. The hunt ended with a sack of squirrels constrained only by the limit of the law. But more frequently, I've hunted within the context of a different framework. I am there for the process, not the bag. On such hunts, I tend to come out of the woods with two or three squirrels.

On my farm in northeast Mississippi, I have Bachman's fox squirrels (the ones with the white faces) as well as gray squirrels. The Bachman's fox squirrel is having a fairly rough time throughout its range, so they are rarely shot on my farm and I hardly ever shoot them elsewhere. They're reserved for youth hunters who hunt on my place and for adult guests who have never hunted where this kind of squirrel lives and perhaps have never even seen one. If a fox squirrel is taken from my farm, it is considered a trophy and the hunt (at least the shooting) ends then. There's also a limit of three squirrels per day and twenty-five squirrels per year on my farm (all hunters combined). That's one squirrel harvested per year per acre of forested land. Only five can be fox squirrels. I could probably shoot more from the place, but then I *do* share the squirrels on my farm with hawks and owls who call my place "home." They probably get another twenty to thirty squirrels from my farm each year, perhaps more, and that's absolutely OK with me.

From time to time, a hunting friend picks up the rhythm of this orientation regarding hunting when I share my experiences around campfires, in camps, or just during casual visits. This happened one autumn while I was hunting squirrels over on Davis Island, a huge area that encompasses several hunting clubs along the Mississippi River southwest of Vicksburg, Mississippi.

During a midday break, Nelson Ball, a hunting and fishing partner and good friend of mine, took me to another club member's camp and showed me a fox squirrel with a white face. He said that he'd always wanted to shoot a white-faced fox squirrel. When I told him that these Bachman's fox squirrels lived on my farm and that he should come and hunt there with me, he was beside himself.

For weeks he prepared himself for his squirrel hunt. Nelson is an experienced big game hunter, but this fox squirrel hunt flipped a real switch inside of him. He spent a lot of time on a rifle range sighting in his rifle and reading about the squirrels. When he drove over from his home in central Louisiana, he was as pumped up as a kid on Christmas Eve. He also had his shotgun. His mission, he told me, was to shoot *one* squirrel, just one. And it had to be the right one . . . one for mounting. This was a trophy hunt for Nelson. I don't think he'd have been any less focused or prepared had it been for a trophy bighorn sheep.

Like me, Nelson likes to hunt squirrels with a rifle. But I explained to him that my farm is not a place to safely hunt squirrels with a rifle and that, besides, he would end up with a better trophy for mounting—at least a less shot up trophy—if he used a shotgun with fairly light shot (number 6 or 7½ shot) with a modified choke.

The next morning we drifted across my pasture to a place back in my woods along a fence line where I knew a couple of big Bachman's fox squirrels lived among some huge oaks. I oriented Nelson to the area and told him where he'd likely see the squirrels. Then I left him to his task and started rambling to and through a scope of woods on the other end of my farm. I wasn't very focused on shooting that morning. I just watched the day unfold around me. It's the sort of thing a landowner does to reconnect with the land. I poked around my ponds, kicked half-heartedly at a couple of brush piles, watched some ducks on my neighbor's pond, and then, perhaps two hours later, began rambling back to Nelson's hunting area. I was within a hundred yards of him when I heard him shoot.

As I approached Nelson I found him sitting beside a tree with his big white-faced Bachman's fox squirrel laid out in front of him. He was gently wiping a couple of tiny drops of blood from the squirrel. I heard Nelson take a couple of deep breaths and then saw him wipe his eyes. Here was a man almost sixty years old, sitting in the woods with a dead squirrel, an old shotgun, and a tear on his cheek. Then he looked up at me and said, "Don, I think this was one of the finest, if not *the* finest hunt, in my life. I saw a gray squirrel and then there were two fox squirrels. I just watched them and took my time deciding which one was to be my trophy. What an experience . . . what a great experience."

These words from a man who is one of the finest deer hunters I know and who hunts one of the finest deer hunting places in the United States stunned me momentarily. I was glad to have been able to orchestrate Nelson's fox squirrel hunt, but I'd really had no idea the depth of his focus on getting this trophy animal . . . and how important it was for him. It was more than a trophy. It was a treasure, for both of us. And it solidified a bond that will endure between us as we continue our days afield together.

This woods rambling stuff with squirrel hunting as the prescription does not have to follow the "still hunt and stalk" pattern. It fact, there is another type of squirrel hunting that connects us to the woods and to each other in a very different sort of way. In this style of hunting there are great big men with little tiny dogs that handle this squirrel business in a style all their own.

Once the leaves are off the trees, and especially during late winter after the deer season draws to a close, these men and their dogs gather and off they go adventuring. The little dogs are masters of sight and smell. They locate the squirrels, chase them up trees, bark "treed" to let the hunters know that a squirrel is in a tree, and then keep an eye peeled in case the squirrel decides to switch trees (it's called sky-lining). The hunters and dogs position themselves on opposite sides of the tree and then carefully look to find the squirrel. Typically, it is very high and plastered tight to a branch. Searching with binoculars helps. Because the squirrels are usually very high in the tree, shooting is best done with a very tightly choked shotgun or a straight shooting .22 rifle.

It is this kind of squirrel hunting that the Mississippi Wildlife Federation uses in its annual program to help connect kids to the heritage of small game hunting. After an orientation session on wildlife management, squirrel ecology, and gun safety, the kids are split into groups of hunters, each with a dog and dog handler. One of the adults in the group carries the gun. When a squirrel is treed, the gun is passed to the kid who is in line to do the shooting. Nobody has to be quiet. You can kick logs, slosh in the water, talk with your friends, crunch leaves, and snap sticks as much as you want. There's no pressure on the kids. Everybody is there to have a good time and a good time is had by all. Typically, on an afternoon hunt, three or four squirrels are shot and the young hunters are thrilled. There is no score. There's no reference to the bag limit. There are no measurements. But there are incredible trophies. There's woods rambling, excitement, dogs, guns, and their parent or guardian to share the experiences with them.

After the hunt, the kids are shown how to skin and dress the squirrels while a squirrel dinner is prepared for them. Eating squirrels at sunset, surrounded by seasoned hunters and a new cadre of younger veterans, with the encroaching night sounds from the woods, the deep memories of an afternoon in the woods with guns and dogs and freedom to ramble—all meld together into a perfect combination that stirs deep currents of a hunter's heart for these youngsters. Like the older hunters, these youngsters too are afflicted with woods rambling syndrome. But unlike us, they can't administer the proper treatment without our help. They're trapped unless we take them with us. So, when we treat ourselves for woods rambling syndrome, remember that there are kids who are also suffering from it. The kid that you throw into the truck along with your other essential gear doesn't take up much space. They also like to carry sacks of squirrels.

However, if you do this, if you start taking a kid on squirrel hunts, regardless of whether it is a quiet still hunt or a full-tilt-boogy dog hunt, your woods rambling syndrome will become increasingly worse over time and be increasingly more difficult to control. You'll have to go squirrel hunting more and more and more in order to address the debilitating symptoms. You'll start buying new guns specifically for squirrel hunting. Your box stands over green fields will start to deteriorate. In fact, if you're over fifty years old, you may forget where they are! You'll make up excuses as to why you can't go on those "adults only" hunts for other stuff.

The whole business of taking the kid hunting becomes an obsession. In fact, you eventually face the truth and finally admit that you can't go squirrel hunting alone anymore. There is no support group to help you with your situation. The affliction can get to be so bad that you can, in fact, if you're not careful, become a nuisance to your family, your neighborhood, and perhaps to local scout troops as you try to rustle up a young hunting partner.

As the affliction advances, as you lose the struggle with woods rambling syndrome by taking young hunters on squirrel hunts with you (and you *will* lose the struggle), you need to be fully aware that by so doing you are helping to ensure the future of hunting. So, *do not hunt squirrels,* and especially *do not take kids squirrel hunting* if you don't want this to happen.

OK. You've been warned.

Old Brown Dog

Fog lay thick in the predawn December darkness as I parked my pickup truck at the end of the gravel road leading to my farm. The morning was incredibly still. The sound of a barred owl down by the creek and the bawling of a distant hound on the trail of something deep in the woods were muffled by the stillness.

It was a morning for critters to prowl . . . a "possum" morning. During the ten-minute drive from my house out to the farm, along the county road wet and glistening, with my old mix-breed shepherd dog "Brownie" in the truck with me, and before turning onto the gravel road leading to my farm, I'd seen several of the rascals, as well as a couple of raccoons, a skunk, and three deer. Brownie had seen the deer and whined with excitement as they crossed the road in front of us.

There's something about a foggy winter morning before sunrise that makes wildlife move differently, slower, and, it seems to me, somewhat more recklessly. In addition to the live critters I'd seen that morning on the way to my farm, there had been two possums, one raccoon, and one skunk freshly killed on the road. I'd stopped for the "coon," found it to be in good condition, and tossed it into the bed of my truck. Once skinned, stretched, fleshed, and dried, the hide would be worth twenty dollars . . . enough (back then) for a week's worth of gas for my truck.

In the thick fog, the scent of the skunk I'd passed hung heavily in the air. It wasn't something I minded. I guess I'm sort of strange in this regard, but the smell of a skunk is not displeasing to me, just as long as it is not at close range and I'm not the target. The deer I'd seen were right out *in* the road and were in no hurry to get out of it. In fact, I'd had to slow down to almost a crawl before they decided to get out of my way. Even then, they just walked off to the edge of the pavement, stiffed-legged and somewhat arrogant. Brownie made it clear to me that he was more than willing to help them remember their wild genes and that he would be answering the call of his own wild genes in doing so. As the deer ambled across the road, that dog ended up right on top of me as I was trying to drive. I had to push him away and back to his side of the truck.

As I pulled up to the gate of my farm, the small wood-frame house beside the gate was adorned with Christmas lights of all colors. The lights are there all year long, but during the Christmas season, they're plugged in . . . twenty-four hours a day. My neighbor Charles Daley owns this house and lives there. A tattered and faded American flag hung wet and loose from the pole next to where he had his tractor parked.

I was careful not to slam my truck's door, rattle the gate, or make any other loud sounds that might disturb Charles and his family. It was so quiet that I could hear occasional drops of water dripping from the eaves of his house and into an old bucket. Water was beaded up on the turnip greens in his patch beside my gate, making the leaves glisten under the glow of the security light by his house. I had a standing invitation from Charles to take advantage of that turnip green patch, and so I made a mental note to be sure to pick some after my morning hunt.

Charles's extended family has established a small community of about a dozen homes and house trailers scattered along and just beyond the half-mile-long gravel road leading to my farm gate. The Daley Community is framed and defined by land that has been in Charles's family since the family was emancipated from slavery after the Civil War. Although collectively it is a fairly large block of land, around fifty acres, with every new generation the land has been carved into smaller and smaller portions, with most of the families now owning only a couple of acres each—enough for a house, a garden, and a pen for a horse or other livestock. Charles's passion is raising cattle. But because the family land has been carved up over the course of 150 years, he only has around fifteen acres behind his house for his livestock. This is Mississippi culture: family, history, life lived close to the land, inextricable with it . . . regardless of shifts in economies, politics, or life stations . . . we hold onto it tightly, all of us, but each in his own way.

So, when I bought my farm back in the mid 1990s, Charles and I struck a deal. He agreed to watch my gate to be sure that potential intruders to my land are held a bay. In return, he was granted haying rights to around twenty acres of pastureland on my place. This helps him get the hay he needs to keep his cattle fed during winter, and it helps ensure that when I enter my farm—my sanctuary—I will be the first person on it since the last time I was there. Just knowing *that* is a treasure to me every time I walk past my gate.

There are no other roads or gates to the place and all of the surrounding property is in large tracts that are strictly posted and guarded by their owners. These landowners are good neighbors.

We respect each other's property and have mutual agreements that we can cross fences if necessary to retrieve shot deer and other game, straying livestock, straying dogs, straying children, and other critters.

My neighbors do not manage their land for wildlife. They are cattle farmers and timber producers. Because I *do* manage for wildlife, my farm has over the years become a fabulous place to hunt and also provides a nucleus of sorts for wildlife to spill over into the surrounding properties. My neighbors appreciate that, especially during deer season. They hunt the edges of my land, and that's fine with me. And I have no hesitation when a deer is just across a fence line or when there are ducks on their ponds. It is a perfect setup . . . an absolute treasure.

Hunting season on my farm starts in September with dove hunting, then moves to archery for deer, then to squirrels, then rifle season for deer, then to duck hunting on my ponds, and finally, at the end of the season, in February, just before fishing kicks in, I revert back to squirrels and engage in an occasional rabbit hunt. I love it all. I love the fast darting flights of doves on dusty late summer afternoons. I love the quiet and closeness of archery hunting and the way an arrow swishes just before the "click-click" of blades cutting ribs on both sides. I love the scratching of squirrels on bark, the crashing of branches overhead, the stalk, the sharp report of a .22 rifle, and the thump as Mr. Squirrel hits the deck from his perch high in an old water oak tree. I love the magic of deer materializing during the last fleeting moments of light as twilight settles on the land, and the sparkle of sunshine on frost as a buck slips out of the brush and into the clearing . . . the "boom" of a high-powered rifle and the way a deer looks, stretched out, slick, beautiful, and sleek as you walk up to it on the ground after the shot and tracking . . . and the sweet animal smell of the deer as it is dragged to a spot for field dressing on a cold morning. I especially love the whistle and rush of wings as ducks come to decoys on my ponds, and the way my old shotgun seems to shoot itself, with ducks folding and hitting the water and me wondering how in the world a man my age can still hit a wood duck twisting through the trees. I am in love with it all. And my little Mississippi farm has through the years wrapped itself around my heart. It truly is my sanctuary.

Although there is an open invitation to friends and family members to join me on my hunts in the sanctuary, few take me up on it. So my hunts are almost always solitary affairs, except during duck season, when my dog becomes my companion. And so it was this quiet, foggy December morning. I opened the door to my truck and called softly to Brownie, telling him to unload. He hit the ground and started his routine of sniffing and marking around the gate. I grabbed my shotgun, gently and quietly shut and locked the door of my truck, and slipped through the gap between fence poles beside my gate. As I began my walk across the pastures to my duck ponds, I thought about how strange it was to be hunting with a dog such as this. Here I was, a seasoned duck hunter, with a yellow mutt with absolutely no idea of his lineage. He does not have oily hair so has to wear a neoprene jacket to stay warm. He weighs only about fifty pounds (small for a retriever) but is powerfully built. He has big shoulders, a fine square head (but pointy nose), and a long tail for a rudder. He's the sort of dog you'd expect to hang around a farmhouse, one that probably lives under some porch or out in a barn, but not the sort of dog that you take hunting. He's the sort of dog used to make sure that strange cars and strange people get barked at. He's the sort of dog that will kill a rat or keep raccoons out of a corn patch. But he's not the sort of dog that you'd ever think about if you were planning on some big hunt way off to the west in the Delta region of the state, where duck hunting is a sort of religion. But here he was, with me on that foggy December morning, and we both were heading for a duck hunt and both of us had confidence in the other partner.

Brownie came into my life as a puppy in a cardboard box during an elementary school outdoor PTA event one Saturday morning many years ago, when my sons were very small boys and my daughter was still a baby. One of the school's teachers had a litter of puppies that she was trying to unload. Free fuzzy puppies in a cardboard box with kids and parents in a festive mood are a good mix for such a mission. Mississippi schoolteachers are smart. I ended up with one of the puppies in the truck that morning. My oldest son, Robert, had his arms around that puppy and wouldn't turn loose. We named him Brownie, but he didn't have a brown hair on him. Rather, he was a golden yellow with a bit of black mixed in around his tail. But Brownie it was . . . regardless. Brownie was added to our family as a "kid" dog, whose purpose was that of filling in the spaces that my old duck dog, a huge chocolate-colored Labrador retriever named Tori, left blank. The big Lab, though friendly, was not a dog inclined to play. The kids could crawl all over him and even ride him like a horse, but he would not play. And my kids needed a dog to play with . . . a dog to dig holes with in the yard, to chase each other around the trees, and to lay with in the grass, watching bugs.

But during training periods for the Lab, the new puppy watched and learned. He'd sit patiently on the patio as I worked with the Lab . . . just watching. I did not take him seriously. Sometimes I'd call him and include him in the activities. He especially enjoyed going out to my farm. Out there he was fine chasing sticks in the pond and seemed to handle the commands pretty well, but I did not want to mess up hunts by having him along. After all, he was a mongrel, a mutt, with questionable linage and no pedigree at all. And yet he had something in his heart that was undeniable. He knew he was a hunter. I knew it also, but would not admit it. He'd use his nose to find sticks lost in the tall grass and bushes. He mastered basic commands—mark, back, fetch, over, whoh, hi-on—just by watching the old dog. He even picked up hand signals. But for a couple of years I ignored the obvious. I took him on dove hunts because dove hunts are parties and really not serious affairs (at least not to me). However, that yellow shepherd mutt took it seriously and did a tremendous job finding lost doves for us. He'd get into the thickest of brambles and, eventually, out he'd come, dove in mouth. This is unusual for even the finest blooded retrievers because dove feathers tend to come off in a dog's mouth and dogs generally don't like it when this happens. But it didn't seem to bother Brownie. He loved the hunt. He loved the sound of guns. He loved to find downed birds and bring them to the hunter. A shepherd mutt, a yellow shepherd mutt . . .

Finally, after considerable encouragement and arm-twisting from the home front (particularly from my wife, who couldn't stand to hear Brownie whining when the Lab and I took off together for our duck hunts), I relented and took Brownie with me on a duck hunt. But I was skeptical, very skeptical. Would he stay still as ducks circled? Would he bark? Could I trust him? I just couldn't be sure. So I tied him to a tree back in some thick bushes behind me on a small island out in the pond and then took position. The old Lab sat at my side, as still as a log, with just his eyes moving. I was just as still. Just before the sun rose, ducks started moving. I could see flocks flying over the trees beyond the pond and across the pasture. A pair of wood ducks wheeled by, but they were gone before I had a chance to get my gun up. Then a flock of gadwalls started circling my decoys. Gadwalls are suspicious ducks. They circled and circled and circled, looking for *anything* that might possibly be wrong . . . a decoy with ice on top reflecting sunlight, an old spent shotgun shell laying out in the mud, a dark shadow in the grass, even a muddy foot print. These gadwalls kept on circling, once, twice, three times, wheeling far out over my pasture, then coming back around, again and again. Finally, convinced that all was in proper order, they came floating in on stiff, cupped wings, feet stretched out, wind whispering through feathers, coming in as slick as cream. I let them come on in until the first duck was just about to touch the water. Then I shot at the duck most distant from me, then the next in line, and finally the first duck that had almost landed, empting my old pump gun—bang, bang, bang—and, wonder of all wonders, three ducks lay belly-up on the water out in the middle of my pond. It was one of those special events that is etched in my mind forever. I just stood there, looking at the ducks out on the pond and at my old Lab, who was looking back up at me . . . just as surprised at my performance as I was (he knew this sort of thing was not the normal thing for his hunting companion). But he was enough of a gentleman not to let on, not now with that "puppy" Brownie back in the bushes watching the entire affair. For this I was grateful. No sir, old Tori acted like this was just standard routine, and I played along with him.

I hollered, "Back," and out he went, all one hundred pounds of him, cutting a wake across the pond like a bear. He brought in the first duck, delivered it to hand, and then I hollered again, "Back."

Out he went again, and soon duck number two was in hand. Then I looked back at Brownie. The yellow mutt shepherd was trembling with excitement but holding fast to position, sitting tight. I hadn't expected this. I'd figured that he would be chewing at the rope or jerking around. But no, he was behaving himself. His behavior was something totally unexpected . . . a second miracle of sorts for the morning (following the first miracle of three ducks with three shots). So I tied up the Lab and untied the shepherd. Brownie held tight. I said, "Back," and that mutt hit the water like a field trial champion, churned his way out across the pond to the duck, and did a picture-perfect retrieve, right into my hand. It was then that I realized what I had. And from that day on Brownie was part of my duck hunts.

Three years later the old Lab finally called it quits and is resting now under an oak overlooking the pond where we hunted ducks together. We all miss the old gentleman, but the hunts continue. Now it is just Brownie and me. And, with the passage of time, that yellow mutt has moved into the ranks of first-class duck dogs. His heart is full of it. And the more he hunted, the better he got at it. But there's more . . .

On that foggy December morning, I went through the farm gate, pump gun slung over my shoulder and coffee cup in hand. The ground was squishy under my wader boots as I walked across my farm back to the wild brushy pond down in the woods where wood ducks like to come on winter mornings. As I walked, I could hear owls in the woods and occasionally a faint rush of wings as early ducks moved restlessly across the sky.

Slipping down into the woods to the wild brushy pond, I took my position beside a gnarled tupelo gum tree. Brownie took his position beside the stump he always sits by. I sipped on my coffee, said my morning prayer, and then loaded the gun. Decoys were not necessary. The wood ducks come to that pond regardless.

A few minutes later, as the sky turned from black to a steely gray, a woodcock came flittering overhead. That woodcock is my timer, letting me know that ducks will soon be on their way. True to form, less than five minutes later, there was a squeal and a rush of wings as wood ducks came twisting in through the trees to land on the pond. I shot twice and knocked down one duck. It was a cripple and it landed on the far side of the pond. Brownie was after it in a heartbeat. I followed as closely as possible. But it disappeared in brush and fog. I could hear Brownie in the thick bushes, snuffling around, trying to find that duck. That crippled duck was a runner and was making fast tracks, getting as far away from the pond and us as possible. Eventually, however, I heard a flapping of wings and brush breaking. A few moments later Brownie emerged with a very much alive drake wood duck. Without Brownie, this duck would never have been brought to bag.

After collecting that duck, I decided to leave the brushy wild pond down in the woods. Brownie and I crawled up on top of the levee of the bigger pond. I wanted to see if there were any snipe on the mud flats around the edge of the big pond. As I circled the pond, Brownie lagged behind. Finally, I looked back and here he came with another wood duck. Apparently I had *not* missed with my second shot. So here I was with two ducks—a limit, in fact, for wood ducks—and it was all Brownie's fault. Without that dog, I'd have been duckless that morning.

I praised him for a job well done and told him that for a reward we'd slip down into the woods and see if we could get a squirrel. I found a feed tree and settled down at its base, with Brownie laying down beside me. We'd been sitting for perhaps ten minutes.

I spotted a gray squirrel and was hoping that eventually it would meander over our direction. Then I looked through the woods and saw a group of three deer moving. Brownie also saw them. Although alert, and very tense, he didn't move. After a few moments, I decided to release Brownie just to see what he would do. I expected him to chase the deer and bark, but he did not chase, nor did he bark. Rather, his shepherd heritage took over and he circled around the deer. Then, slowly and gently, he *herded* them right past me—not fifteen yards away! The deer never saw me. Their attention was directed at the yellow dog gently moving side to side a hundred yards behind them. I didn't have deer loads for my gun that morning, but it would have been easy to have gotten one of those deer if I'd had the right loads. I was amazed at Brownie's herding skills. It wasn't anything I'd ever seen him do before, and certainly nothing that he'd been trained to do. A dog herding deer? Who ever thought or heard of such a thing. A dog chasing deer, yes, trailing deer, yes . . . but herding them?

After the deer episode we went looking for rabbits. We kicked brush and brush piles, but found no rabbits. Suddenly, Brownie started acting funny. I'd never seen him act like that . . . low to the ground, tail beating rapidly. I thought, OK, he's got a rabbit now—get ready. Then he stopped and leaned forward and stiffened like some setter, pointer, or Brittany. Brownie was on a solid point! I said to myself that what I was witnessing could not possibly be true. But regardless, I stepped forward, gun ready, looking at the ground, ready for the rabbit to tear out from its hiding place. All I had was number 4 steel shot, a little big for rabbits, but I figured I'd let it get out a little way before shooting and it would be OK. I took two steps and, instead of a rabbit, a covey of quail erupted in front of Brownie's nose. As they fanned out in front of me I shot and one of the birds fell. Brownie ran to it immediately. He'd never seen a quail before and just stood there sniffing it. I shouted a command, "Fetch." Brownie looked at me, then at the bird, gently picked it up, and fetched it to my hand. *Then* he started hunting singles. I just couldn't believe it. Suddenly, he locked up again on point. Still not believing what was happening, I kicked in front of him and a single quail got up. I shot but this time missed. It didn't matter. The magic of what had just happened with this old yellow mutt dog was flooding the world around me. Ducks, deer, and now *quail*. What *couldn't* this dog do?

We tried for a while to locate the other quail, but they'd vanished on the other side of a creek, on the property of one of my neighbors who I knew was deer hunting that morning. I didn't want to go over there for fear of messing up his deer hunt. So I just called it quits for the morning, whistled for Brownie, and started back toward the truck.

As we walked back to the truck together, with our two ducks and the quail, I kept thinking about how lucky I was that there were no bear or cougar on my farm. Had there been, I'm convinced that Brownie would have been right in the thick of them that morning. And all I had with me were duck loads. What a morning! What an absolutely incredible morning with an incredible dog!

As I write this, Brownie is stretched out on a rug just a few feet from me in our living room. He's now an old dog. He's slow, and it hurts him to move very fast. He gets stiff and it takes him awhile to limber up. When I go hunting now, I'm afraid to let him go out into an icy pond for a duck anymore. But if I try to sneak out of the house early in the morning with a shotgun to go duck hunting without him, it breaks his heart and also breaks mine. His whines are more than I can stand. The hunt is in his heart. He is truly a hunter. I do not know where his hunting genes came from, but he has proven to me that if the hunt is in a dog's heart (or a person's), it will come out. Just open the gate . . .

Rare and Precious Gifts

A WHISPER OF WIND RUFFLED THE WATER AND CAUSED THE grass along the mudflat to move gently. Killdeers and other shorebirds called. In the half-light of dawn I saw the shadow of a deer moving along the edge of the flooded area that spread before me. A muskrat nipped at vegetation along the shoreline. A fish swirled in the murky shallows. I was lost in thought when suddenly two wood ducks whipped by in a rush of wing beats, the hen filling the stillness of the morning with her eerie cry, bringing me to full attention as a duck hunter. It was mid-September, near the end of the season for hunting resident Canada geese, and the beginning of the early season for teal.

I was hunting alone with my chocolate Labrador retriever, Tori, on a large tract of land called Blocker's Bottoms, about ten miles from my home in east central Mississippi. Blocker's Bottoms is located along the northeastern border of Noxubee National Wildlife Refuge and is managed as pasture for cattle and as wetlands for wildlife. It is private land and subsequently off limits to the general public. Additionally, and because of its connection with a fairly remote and difficult-to-access part of the refuge, the area is incredibly rich in wildlife, and seasonally this is particularly so with respect to waterfowl and shorebirds. Blocker's Bottoms is such a large area, and so far from the normal passages of people, that when you're out rambling across this landscape you're surrounded by a primeval quiet that only the wilder places in Mississippi afford. It is a landscape full of hush, an environment that for outdoor sojourners stretches the body, the senses, and the mind.

I have a good friend, Russell Gaines, who owns a big chunk of Blocker's Bottoms. Like me, he's an avid duck hunter as well as big game hunter. Over the years we've hunted some together and have also worked together to improve fishing in some of his ponds. Our conversations invariably have drifted into the realms of land stewardship, and after a few years he recognized that I needed to have land of my own. So he sold me a beautiful farm where I could practice my profession as a wildlife and fisheries manager from private and personal perspectives, where I could find sanctuary and refuge when the world closed in on me, and where I could teach my kids how to fish and hunt and connect with the rhythms of the earth. But beyond this incredible sensitivity, my friend also gave me access to his other properties, including Blocker's Bottoms, so that I'd have larger spaces to roam.

Blocker's Bottoms is not a place where I would ever go, or would even ask to go, during the regular duck season or during the deer season (although I have hunted late season ducks as well as deer there, but only with Russell). I know that hunts for ducks and deer are sacred times for him, and I also know that he too needs his very personal, very private connections with the lonely land. So I confine my activities in Blocker's Bottoms to September, when my friend typically is not focused on hunting.

A couple of days before teal season opened, one very special year back when the dog and I both had an overdose of grit and vinegar in our craw, I called Russell and asked permission to hunt down in the bottoms. My friend said, "Have at it," just as he always had in years past. So the following afternoon I drove my truck out to the bottoms to have a look. After parking the truck by Russell's barn up on a hill overlooking the bottoms, I walked down to the place where I usually hunt teal. When I finally got there I was pleased to see that beavers had dammed up a low spot and that rain from the remnants of a recent hurricane had flooded about fifty acres of grass and overgrown crops that had been planted for wildlife. The water was receding very slowly. I could see a fringe of mud around the periphery of the area and predicted that within a few days the mud flats would be perfect . . . just the sort of habitat that's a magnet for teal.

It was a beautiful place on that late summer day. I could smell the deep, dank odor of rotting vegetation mixed with mud. Cicadas hummed. A hawk cruised by. Turtles basked on old logs. The willows and buttonbush framed the wetland, while in the distance I could see the tall timber that marked the boundary of the refuge. I took a deep breath. It was so quiet. It was so still . . . shimmering in the late afternoon sun. It was the Deep South at its finest. So I just stood there, perhaps for an hour, maybe more, it didn't matter, soaking it all in, waiting, hopeful, watching the sun set over the trees along the refuge boundary. And then as I watched, a flock of about a dozen teal whirled by and settled on the water about fifty yards from me. They'd obviously ridden the cool front that had drifted down from the north a couple of days before. My hunter's heart quickened at the sight of them. The magic was there and would still be there when the season opened.

The walk down to the flooded area had been pretty tough and the walk back was equally as tough. The grass was nearly shoulder high and, as a native of the Deep South, I knew that I had to be very careful about where I put my feet. Blocker's Bottoms is a place that is most definitely cottonmouth and copperhead country. To "grease the skids" so that my early morning treks in the dark to the shooting hole would be a bit quicker, and to make life a little more snake proof, I cranked up my tractor the following day, drove it from my farm down to the bottoms, and bush hogged a trail through the tall weeds. I started mowing at the top of a hill where I usually parked my truck and then worked along the edge of the pasture to where an old fence line bounded the flooded area. As I whacked out my narrow trail along the fence, I saw three teal wheel around the area and finally come to rest on the water next to one of the emerging mud flats. The teal season would open the next morning . . . and I was ready.

Sunrise was still more than an hour away on opening morning when I shut off the truck's engine by the barn. I let the dog out of the truck so that he could stretch and sniff and attend to other necessary business, poured myself another cup of coffee from my beat-up thermos, and then just stood there for a while, looking out into the darkness before me . . . imagining the flooded bottoms and the restless teal getting ready for their morning flights.

I was like a kid on Christmas morning, a kid trying to stay in bed until called but all the while about to explode, knowing that beneath the tree were delights almost beyond imagining. After about ten minutes of piddling around by my truck and trying to be calm and patient, I had to admit to myself that the resolve of a child is greater than that of a duck hunter. I couldn't stand it any longer. So I surrendered to my frailty and passions, gulped down the last swallow of coffee, reached into the back compartment of the truck's cab, and pulled out my old pump gun, a slick and scarred veteran of many years. I checked the gun by habit to be sure that it was unloaded, slung it across my shoulder, grabbed my small sack of duck decoys, stuffed in two goose decoys, whistled up the dog, and was on my way.

With flashlight bobbing, casting its tiny circle of light on the trail, I tromped through the darkness, the heavy dew soaking my cotton trousers and my worn leather boots and the sweet smell of cut grass flooding my senses. Although it was cool that morning, it was still too warm to wear hip boots or waders, especially considering that I had a fairly long walk back to the flooded area. But because of this I needed to be extra careful regarding snakes. Fortunately, I only had to sidestep one of the rascals along the trail that morning.

Once I got to my crossing spot on the fence line, I slung the decoy sack over to the other side of the fence, opened the action of my gun, carefully placed the gun on the ground pointing away from me, and crawled under the lowest strand of barbed wire, slithering like and probably among the snakes. Then I gathered my stuff and was off to my setup spot: a small point of mud flat that had a nice clump of buttonbush on it to serve as my blind. As I approached the point I could hear Canada geese gabbling out there in the darkness someplace in the flats but couldn't see them.

After putting out my decoys I slipped back to my blind in the bushes and whistled for the dog. I could hear him splashing around out by the decoys, and finally I could see his shadow as he came up through the mud to join me. Then the wait began. I think that during the time I stood there waiting for legal shooting time there were probably no less than two complete ice ages. Finally shooting time arrived and I loaded my gun with number 4 steel shot.

Standing there in the shadows of the bushes, with shorebirds all around me, geese gabbling in the distance, and a sunrise developing behind me, the world was transformed into something magic. A quiet settled upon my heart and stilled my spirit. Another pair of wood ducks wheeled in and landed among my decoys. Both were young drakes with drab markings. Then I heard a faint rustling of wings, looked up, and saw a flock of roseate spoonbills drifting in. They were gorgeous! I'd only seen spoonbills once before in the wild, and that had been a long time ago, back during my college days on an ornithology field trip down to the Texas coast. There were nearly two dozen of them now about to land right in front of me. They came down so softly, stood momentarily looking around, and then started wading and feeding their way to a back corner of the flooded area.

I was transfixed at the sight of these magnificent birds, so much so that I failed to notice a flock of teal that had slipped in on me. When I turned around there were five teal swimming among my decoys. I got my gun ready. But they were preoccupied with feeding and didn't notice me. It was obvious that I needed to move to get them to fly, and so I began to walk slowly toward them. They didn't see me at first, but then perked up, hesitated for a moment, and flushed.

My old gun went to my shoulder as if it had a mind of its own and seemed to shoot all by itself. One teal hit the water. Then I pumped the gun and held on another teal. At my shot two more teal came down. One hit the water dead and lay floating belly up, but the other was crippled and flapping away across the water, trying to get to a hiding spot in the brush. Tori ripped across the water and mud, and after a bit of a chase, grabbed that crippled duck and brought him back to me.

So there I was, less than ten minutes into the opening of the teal season, and I already had three ducks. I was allowed only one more. Now I really had to be careful because teal often fly so close together that more than one is hit with a single shot, just like what had already happened only moments before. I didn't want to risk going over my limit.

My shots at the teal stirred up the geese. Just as my dog brought that crippled teal back to me the geese went berserk with wild honking and a beating of wings. It was then that I got my first glimpse of them. They'd been roosting just a little more than a hundred yards from me but obscured by vegetation. As they cleared the vegetation and gained some altitude, a couple of them saw my two goose decoys mixed in with the ducks decoys and pulled the rest of the flock with them to come investigate. They were coming straight for us! Obviously, and in spite of the fact that the goose season was nearly over, it seemed that these geese had not been hunted, at least not much. I quickly reloaded with heavy goose loads.

Tori sensed what was about to happen, and I could see him quiver with excitement. Both of us hunkered down into the brush as deeply as possible, not looking up, waiting and waiting and waiting until the geese were almost right overhead. Then I stood up, held on one of the geese, fired, and down it came, a huge, tumbling monster plucked from the sky. It hit with a crash next to us, breaking small branches from a willow tree beside us as it fell. After that shot the other geese made a wide circle out across the bottoms and, for reasons known only to the geese, came back around and crossed just outside of the decoys, about thirty yards in front of me. I couldn't believe it! But I was ready. I held on the goose at the head of the flock, pulled my lead about six feet in front of it, and shot. The goose threw its neck back as the charge connected and came down hard on the mud flat, sending mud and water flying as it hit the deck. The other geese, realizing now what was going on, tightened their formation and quickly got beyond range, filling the morning with their calls until eventually, after several minutes, they were beyond earshot.

Tori had already rushed out to the goose on the flat by the time I'd collected myself, calmed my breathing, and reloaded for ducks. But he was still a young dog back then and he'd never seen or retrieved anything so big. He just rambled around the goose for a minute or so, trying to figure out what to do with this thing before him. At first he tried to get the standard hold around the body of the bird, but that was impossible. Then he tried grabbing a foot. But the goose's wings dug into the mud like anchors. Finally, he grabbed a wing and dragged the bird back across the mud to me. It was just too big for even a ninety- pound dog to carry.

About that time another flock of eight to ten teal roared in. They were so tightly packed that I held my shot. I waited until they were about to land, then jumped up, waved my gun a little, and the flock came apart. One duck headed off in the direction of the spoonbills that were now a couple of hundred yards away. I swung on that teal, fired, and missed. Then another came ripping by overhead. I led it as far as I could, pulled the trigger, and it's wings folded. That was it. I had my four-duck limit and two big Canada geese. I glanced at my watch. It was 7:45.

As quickly as I could I went out to retrieve my decoys. I wanted to leave before the remaining ducks in the area were spooked. Since I only had six duck and two goose decoys out, it didn't take very long to cram them into the sack. Then I hid the decoys back in the bushes so they'd be available for future hunts, grabbed my gun, put one goose and two teal on each side of my duck stringer, slung the birds across my shoulder, called the dog, and headed back to the truck. It took me about twenty minutes to slosh my way back to the fence through the mud and follow my trail back up from the bottoms to the top of the hill where I'd parked my truck. I was glad that it wasn't further. One goose weighed about fifteen pounds and the other weighed nearly twelve pounds. They were *big* birds.

Once I got to the truck I put the birds in the truck's bed, stowed my gun behind the back seat, poured myself a cup of coffee, and, leaning against my truck, spent a few minutes just looking out across Blocker's Bottoms. The sun had turned the world orange and pink. There was a cool breeze. A crow cawed. A redwing blackbird filled the air with its summer song. A couple of doves whistled by. Down on the bottoms I could see teal buzzing like bumblebees over the grass and landing in little bunches out on the shallow water flats. I thought about the magnificent hunt I'd just had. All the ingredients had come together and the magic had certainly been there.

But from within my reflections there came another overwhelming thought that really wasn't a thought at all but something whose source was much, much deeper. It helped me understand that it wasn't the hunt, the place, or even the incredible beauty of the day that were my greatest blessing. Rather it was the rare and precious gift of a friendship that had opened the way for me to be out there on that property as a hunter.

And in those reflections I was reminded that hunting is a privilege, not a right, and that when we are invited to hunt on someone's land, we as hunters are more than mere guests. We become caretakers of an awesome trust as stewards of the land, the wildlife resources, and our heritage as hunters. That trust is essential and absolutely must be respected if the future of our sport, hunting as we know it, is to be ensured. That trust can never be betrayed. It is the trust above all that is and will remain the core element of our legacy . . . how we remember . . . how we are remembered.

I took a deep breath, walked back to look again at my ducks and the two geese, and carefully arranged their feathers so that they wouldn't get rumpled on the way home. Then I called the dog to load up. I knew where I'd be the next morning and, in fact, every morning for the next couple of weeks. After that the teal would be gone, on their way to points further south, and my focus would shift to other ventures, other hunts, other places. But I knew that the images of these days on Blocker's Bottoms would linger in my mind and that the echoes of the hunts would linger in my soul.

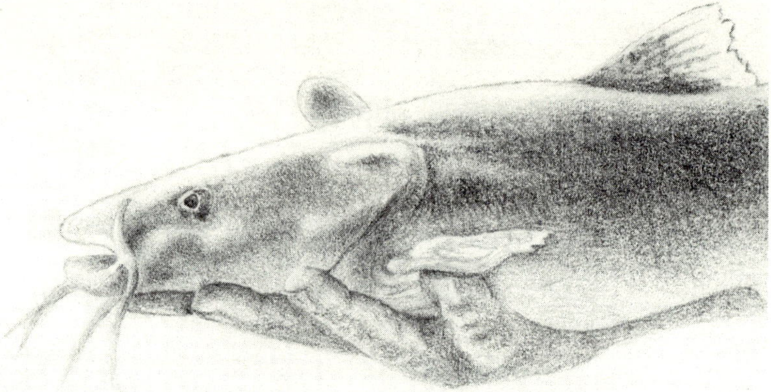

The River's Song

MOST PEOPLE TEND TO INTERACT WITH RIVERS IN WAYS THAT don't work. A river is not about counting things or measuring things or storing things or saving things. It is silly, but we insist on doing it. I do it. I really don't have a lot of choice in this regard because in the other world, the world beyond rivers and river time, I'm a university professor who earns a living doing science. I do research about rivers and river fisheries. But even as I do science, I know that science is a shallow means for understanding rivers and that it cannot capture what rivers are all about. Poets do a better job of it. So do musicians. Commercial fishermen and fur trappers and some canoers do it the best. Science may help us to know more about rivers. But it does very little in helping us to understand them. There's a difference.

My profession as a scientist in natural resources opens the door for me to be on the rivers as a fisherman. As a fisheries biologist I use the commercial gear of the river people. I fish for the commercial species, the catfishes, buffalo fishes, and gars. I run my nets and lines and drive my boats. Mud and muck and fish slime and blood cover me by the end of the day. Ropes burn my hands. I am either scorched by sun or frozen stiff from handling icy gear. Sometimes the river is flush with the colors of new life and changing seasons.

Sometimes the river is gray and mean and hostile. Sometimes it is deep green, lush, and full of mystery.

The river world wraps itself around me. Sandbars flash. I stop and explore and let the quiet surround me and penetrate me. I listen to the sand move under rushing currents, squeaking and shifting. The turtles and herons grace the snags and shallows. Kites and hawks soar overhead. Ducks flush from hidden pockets. Snakes slip from overhanging branches and then twist away on the water's surface as only snakes can do, certainly swimming but in ways that always make me wonder if it is really so or just a race to keep from slipping into the murky depths.

When I was a boy back in the 1960s, my grandmother lived in the little northeast Arkansas community of Whitton, up in Mississippi County, about forty minutes from Memphis, Tennessee. Whitton was about a three-hour drive from my family's home down in North Little Rock. To get to my grandmother's house, we had to cross the St. Francis River near the town of Marked Tree. As we passed over the bridge I'd always look down at the houseboats and at the old flat-bottom fishing boats tethered alongside of them. I dreamed of living on a houseboat like the ones I saw on that river and of prowling the brown waters of a river like the St. Francis in one of those flat-bottom boats. I couldn't imagine a better life.

That murky old river cast its spell on me. After crossing the bridge, my mind would spin away into a mystical world full of commercial fishermen and trappers. I would envision myself at the tiller of an outboard motor, churning the muddy waters, bucking the river's currents, on my way upstream to check my nets or, with gun beside me, heading for some hidden backwater or slough where I could stalk fox squirrels and ducks after checking my traps. I longed for foggy mornings, stormy nights, trotlines, catfish, floods, number 1½ steel traps, skinning knives, sandbars, mud flats, and raw winds.

There was a movie back then entitled *Tammy*. It was a movie about a girl who lived on a houseboat in a river like the St. Francis down in the Deep South somewhere with an old man who was either her grandfather or uncle. As I recall she was a very pretty girl, and there was some nice music (which I still hum occasionally or play on my harmonica). The movie was some sort of love story mixed with a bit of mystery and adventure. I really didn't follow the story, however. My focus was on the ways of people who somehow had been able to create for themselves the life I longed for. When the movie came to our local theater I couldn't tear myself away from it. In fact, one afternoon I watched it over and over and over again until my mother came into the theater looking for me after I'd failed to show up for supper.

I loved the way that the people in the movie moved their houseboats to wherever suited them, tied them to some big sycamore tree along the riverbank, stretched out a trotline, and then had the woods and water and quiet all around them. As I watched the movie, I could almost smell the dankness of river mud and the tart odor of dead gar mellowing on a sandbar in the summertime sunshine. I could almost feel the wind as it rippled the water at midday and the chill of shadows at dusk. I could, in my heart, hear the resonating humming of cicadas in ancient oaks and walnuts and the tonking of rain crows. I knew that the river was where I belonged.

When I mentioned my desire for such a life to my parents and other kinfolks, I was either ignored or given gentle smiles and chuckles. Those who did listen to me told me that river people were castoffs from society, that theirs was a life of poverty and insecurity, and that there was no future for them or for people who followed their ways. They said that I needed to become a doctor or a teacher or some other "respected" professional. I listened, but rejected their perspective and advice. I didn't want a house on a hill. I didn't want an office. I didn't want towns and traffic and grocery stores in shopping centers. I didn't want to be around a lot of people. It seemed to me that the sages around me didn't hear the call from the river's deep currents, and they certainly didn't hear the answering call that swelled from even deeper currents swirling in my heart.

So, after a while, I just kept my mouth shut and thoughts about such a life to myself. The only person who seemed to understand what I was going through was an illiterate sharecropper named Joel D. Linley, who worked for my Uncle Bob on our family farm in Mississippi County. In addition to his skills as a tractor driver and first-class mechanic, Joel D. was a poacher of some fame and a commercial fisherman and trapper. When I mentioned my love for rivers to him, he'd just laugh, but his laugh was different from the laughter of other adults around me. It came deep from down inside of him and seemed to communicate more acceptance than humor . . . as if to say, "OK, if this is what you want, then so be it and climb in. I'll show you how." And he did.

He'd take me to the shed where he hid his illegal fish traps and show me how to stretch them out and bait them. He'd talk about how to catch otter and mink. He'd instruct me on ways to dress gar. He had an old boat and motor and would take me fishing on a chute of the Mississippi River and talk about how to make a boat go where you want it to when in strong currents. Although he couldn't express it in words, he knew the river's song. He sang it with his life. He was one of the river people. I became his shadow whenever I went to visit my grandmother.

River people like Joel D. are indeed out of synchrony with the rest of the world. And good for them! Their time is not world time. Their time is river time. It marks passages that are in fact unknown to the other world or at least unappreciated. World time and river time don't mix. River time is all about rises and falls and seasons and relentless but dynamic energy . . . always coming, always going, always shifting, pulling, pushing, teasing, threatening, enduring. Nothing seems to stay the same.

But there is something very regular about river time . . . and also very constant. We only have to wrap our minds around the proper dimensions of scale, shift our senses, and really listen, not just with ears but with our total being. The river will not shout at us. Its communication is more a whisper, a murmur, a song. It is a song that is relentless, beautiful, rhythmic, and eternal. But to hear the song we must become very still. We must turn off internal dialogue. And we must be very, very honest with ourselves and with the river, because rivers always tell the truth.

We Do It Because

My bed was warm when the alarm went off at 3:00 a.m. and especially so with the softness of my wife snuggled under the blankets next to me. I'd already been awake, however, for more than an hour, thoughts swirling. I could hear the winter wind roaring outside . . . but there didn't seem to be precipitation with it. Rain had been changing to ice when I'd gone to bed. I wondered now how bad the ice storm had been. There was still electricity in the house, so it probably wasn't too bad. And I'd heard no branches cracking. My thoughts shifted. I had nets in the river that had to be run . . . just like yesterday and the day before and last week and the week before and last year and the years before—twenty-two of them now—all in a row. The nets had to be fished. There was no way to back away from that reality. They had to be fished today, regardless.

I forced myself out of bed, dressed quickly, and moved to my kitchen. The first order of business was a cup of coffee. As the water heated, I went to the refrigerator, pulled out two biscuits, slapped a piece of ham, half a slice of cheese, and a dash of Tabasco sauce on both of them, popped them into the microwave oven, set the timer to forty-five seconds, and pushed "Start." By then the water was boiling and I made a cup of instant coffee. Then the oven's bell announced that the biscuits were ready. I took a few minutes to eat one of them and to enjoy the morning's first cup of coffee. The other biscuit I folded in a paper towel. I'd eat it while driving.

I drifted back toward the bedrooms: one last kiss for my sleeping wife, who smiled and then tucked herself back into a nest of blankets and quilts, one last look at my children in their beds (touching them gently so as not to awaken them). Then, quietly walking back to the kitchen, slipping into the rubber boots that I'd brought inside the previous night so that they'd be warm (at least at the start of the day), grabbing the other biscuit, and topping off my coffee cup, I entered my other world.

The wind rattled the icy branches of the dogwood tree beside my driveway and the big pecan tree across the street. Putting my coffee cup on the hood of the pickup truck, I tried to unlock the driver's side door. The key wouldn't enter. It was iced up. So I poured some of my hot coffee on the keyhole and tried again. This time I was successful at unlocking the door, but the door still wouldn't open. So I put my coffee cup back on the hood of the truck, braced myself, and gave the door of my truck a sharp tug. With that tug it broke free from the ice that had sealed it shut.

Leaning across the seat, I put what was left of my cup of coffee into the holder on the truck's dash. Then I climbed inside, adjusted my seatbelt, cranked the truck's engine, turned on the defroster and headlights, let the engine warm for a minute, and backed out into the street in front of my house . . . and into the darkness of a new day. Sunrise was still three hours away. I had a two-hour drive across central Mississippi ahead of me. Although the tree branches, utility lines, and lawns sparkled with ice, the streets themselves were ice free and dry. For this I was thankful. But I knew that I would have to be very careful on the bridges, especially since I'd be pulling a boat. And the icy wind roared.

As I drove through town and across the university campus to the shed where my boat was stored and where my students would be waiting for me, I asked myself the questions that always surge in me when I go to my work on the rivers: "Will this be the day I make my wife a widow? Will this be the day my children lose their father? Will this be the day that the river gets me?" I knew also that during the entire drive from the university, through the hills, and across the Delta to the river these questions would plague me. "Will this be the day . . . ?"

Rivers can and do kill, and especially in winter. Fishing is a dangerous profession regardless of environment, and it can be especially so on rivers. A slip on an icy deck, an unseen snag, a tangled rope, or a fouled net hung on the river bottom can spell doom for the man who fishes the big, murky rivers of the Deep South in winter for a living. Some of us fish for the market. Others fish to feed their families. A few hardy souls are out there fishing for fun. My students and I fish for science and conservation. But we all go regardless of our purposes. We are driven by some energy, some vision, some force indescribable. There is a common denominator among us, something in us that pulls us back to the rivers, day after day, year after year. It is very hard work. Every day on the river is an adventure with new challenges. Even the danger has its allure, and especially during winter.

I love the sting of sleet, the rawness of a north wind, the sucking, surging, swirling power of a river that's trying to freeze but by sheer force of itself cannot. There is something in it all that grabbed my spirit as a child, gave it a hard shake, and now won't let me go. On a raging river in southeastern Arkansas during a storm, with fellow Boy Scouts and two adult leaders, paddling for our lives on the deck of a tiny raft we'd built ourselves, I could not control my shouts of euphoria, nor could I deny that the world of these big rivers was my world. I cannot escape them now . . . nor have I ever wanted to. I must go back to the rivers, again and again and again. And I know in the depths of my soul that someday a river will very likely consume me. In many ways, rivers already have.

If the river doesn't kill by drowning, then it tries by hypothermia. If not by hypothermia, then by injury, concussions from snags unseen, cuts unfelt on frozen limbs . . . until another member of the crew sees what's happened, and by then it can be too late. Boats can tip, and in the icy waters, you have minutes to make your peace. And if you do make it to shore, the backwaters become traps of doom. Ropes seem to have lives of their own and wrap around feet, dragging the unwary into the swirling currents with the weighted nets. The webbing of nets grab uncovered buttons and buckles. Grappling hooks snag clothing and flesh. Moves must be deliberate and synchronized in the confined space of a boat, and especially so on icy decks. Your body becomes too numb to know if the blood on the icy deck or all across your clothes is that of your own, of a fellow crew member, or of the fish. Faces become raw and eyes glazed from the wind and sleet.

Then there are the nets: frozen and stiff with ice as they come onboard. We are forced to kick them to compress them into the growing pile in the boat. They must be compressed or else they eventually become monsters, raising their heads high above the sides of boat, shifting the boat's balance, and setting the stage for capsizing.

And of course the fish . . . always the fish . . . living, wonderful things brought from the depths of the mysterious unseen world we love, treasures from the deep that must be processed quickly and returned to the water alive before they freeze and die. They are as sacraments to us, bridging us with that other world. We're here to ensure life, not take it, but we cannot rush. Deliberation . . . deliberation . . . discipline . . . we're scientists. It must be done correctly, always—never a question regarding the quality of what we bring back home—simple marks on paper, but marks that make all the difference for the future of rivers and the fisheries they support.

In the cab of the truck, there is quiet talk. We do not mention the danger. We all know of it. We stare ahead into the darkness of a lonely highway, listening to the hum of mud-grip tires on pavement, the occasional slight pecking of sleet on the windshield, and the gentle sound of another cup of coffee being poured into a cup. But mostly there is the quiet, the reflection, the reality, the wonder, the incredibly precious pulsations of life in the present tense. Energy swells. And the miles and hours pass.

Ahead, finally, after turning from the highway, churning our way in four-wheel drive along a county road, winching through the mire of one muddy chute after another, four in a row—chutes that once collectively were considered to be part of the so-called road we are on—and then bringing out the chain saw twice to clear fallen trees from last night's storm, is the tiny ramp at the edge of the river.

The sky has shifted from black to steel gray. The wind still roars and so does the river as it rips around a logjam just downstream from the ramp. We can die in that logjam. If for some reason our outboard motor decides to cough and sputter at the beginning of our day, we can be swept into and under that jam. That would be the end. We all know that. But, after taking a hard look at the river, we know that our work for the day is within the bounds of safety and practicality. We've been in and worked successfully in much worse conditions. The conditions we face are, in fact, pretty normal for a Delta river in winter. This is what we do. This is our world as river fisheries biologists. *This* is who we are.

Then it happens . . . it always does . . . a calm settles over us. There is no more fear. There is no time for it. We put on our survival suits—bright orange with reflectors in case we need to be found and rescued, the material of the suits embedded with insulation and floatation, making the suits almost too hot, even on a day like this—carefully securing each suit's legs and arms, each of us checking each other's suit, so that in the event of an accident, there will not be much water inside the suit that could chill to the point of hypothermia. Then we put our boots back on, boots now cold and stiff. We stomp around the truck to loosen them up a little.

Our collective focus now becomes very hard and our movements become deliberate and synchronized. It is almost routine . . . if there *is* routine in river fisheries work. We've launched hundreds of times during this particular project and thousands of times on other projects over the years. Slowly we back the boat down the slippery ramp. It is an old ramp covered by four inches of fresh silt and mud from last week's flood. The tracks and ruts from our work yesterday are still distinct. The truck starts to slide down the ramp, out of control. It along with the boat trailer and the boat would quickly be lost in the river if it were not for the winch cable we had attached from the front bumper of the truck to a big oak at the head of the ramp. The cable tightens but holds. The truck stops slipping. We breathe again.

Slowly, ever so slowly, we release tension on the winch. The trailer goes into the brown water, deeper and deeper. The boat floats and everything stops. Quickly, one member of the team gets into the boat, still secured to the trailer, and works to start the motor. The motor sputters, then catches, and is worked to life. We do not move from our stations. One man is at the controls of the winch and also is standing at ready in case there is a problem with the trailer. Nothing moves. The truck is still running. The driver is at the wheel of the truck, with the door open in case something breaks and the truck ends up in the river, requiring a quick exit. The outboard motor warms as we freeze. But this must be. We face into the wind, all eyes on the boat and the man operating the motor. We cannot risk the outboard motor dying as we move out into the currents. Three minutes later, the student handling the motor gives the thumbs up and we release him and his boat from the trailer. He quickly backs the boat out of the trailer and into the river's current. There is a moment of intensity as he drifts downstream in the current toward the logjam, but then he is off, moving upstream into the current while we winch the truck and the trailer back up from the ramp and secure them on a patch of high, relatively dry ground.

The outboard motor is purring as we walk back down the ramp to the boat. We take our seats and the calm among us deepens. Once on the water, in our boat, we're in the world that we love and know. We take nothing for granted. All onboard are responsible for looking for hidden danger. But this is reflexive and automatic. A peace envelops us as we skim across the water. I can think of nowhere else on earth I'd rather be. I am transformed from being the questioning and fearful man of the predawn hours into a warrior with other warriors, on a mission that we know we can handle successfully. It is always like this. There is no arrogance. Rather, there is tremendous self-confidence, self-confidence founded on experience and competency and respect for the river. We've done this so many times. This is our element.

Our nets are set several miles upstream from the boat ramp. All but the driver turn their backs to the cold wind and sleet. The driver endures. The gray winter woods cling tightly to the riverbank. Sometimes, however, the bank itself loses its grip and slips into the churning water, the trees coming with it. This is, however, essential to the life of the river . . . scour and fill, the introduction of new snags that serve as attachment sites for invertebrates to feed the fish and also as refuge habitat for fishes that are cover oriented. Wild ducks flush and flair as we round the tight bends of the river. Beaver and otter slip into the water and swim before us momentarily before slipping into the murky depths. There are occasional deer and other wildlife along the riverbank. We point at these things but without words. Our faces are frozen and stiff. We cannot talk, even if we wanted to.

Finally we reach the location of our first set. The driver slows the boat and all of us reposition ourselves. A grappling hook on a long line comes into service. The man on the bow deck tosses it out, the rope uncurling beautifully in the direction of the cod-end of the net. It takes three tries before the net is hooked. Slowly, ever so slowly, we bring the net and the boat alongside one another. Then, reaching down, we grab the net webbing with our bare hands and work our way down to the first hoop at the net's mouth. Gloves at this moment would slip and potentially cause accidents. We must have secure holds on the net. The boat drifts below the net as we hang onto the hoop. The force at first is tremendous, and then the tension breaks as the net comes from the water. In the cod-end of the net there is great splashing. The catch is good. There are several buffalo fish, a couple of gar, and three catfish: one nice blue and two medium-sized flatheads. We shout success among us and to the wind and bring the net into the boat. A catch like this warms us even as we freeze.

We let the rope on the net's cod-end keep us in position as we get our equipment ready to process our catch. Each fish, one at a time, is removed from the net, identified as to species, measured, weighed, tagged, and released back into the river. It takes us less than ten minutes to process the catch. The buffalo fish are processed first because they are the most delicate and subject to the most stress from handling. Then come the gar, then other scaly fish, and last are the catfishes. The wet net, the protection from the wind from the boat's high gunnels, and the cool temperature keep the fish from being too stressed. Once all of the fish are processed, we untie the net from whatever structure we'd secured it to when setting it the day before: a root or tree on the stream bank, a snag, sometimes a piece of steel rebar that we bring along with us for such purposes when there is no other structure to tie off on. When it is necessary to use rebar, the rebar is shoved about two feet into the mud of the stream bank and the cod-end rope is tied as low as possible to the rebar, preferably right at ground level in order to keep the rebar from working loose from the action of current on the net.

With the frozen net now crushed flat on the bottom of our boat, we move to our next net and repeat the process. Most nets have fish, but occasionally one does not. We just keep moving along, retrieving our nets, and recording the data until we've processed the entire set of ten nets. These nets were set at one-hundred-meter intervals on opposite sides of the river. This actually is the only difference between what we do as fisheries scientists and what commercial and subsistence fishermen do. We have systematic placement of our nets while the other fishermen look for the best places to set nets. As a result, our catches typically are less than those of other fishermen. But our approach allows us to make comparisons of times and places: years, seasons, different rivers, and different sections of rivers.

By noon our work on the river is finished and we start the trip back to the boat ramp. It takes about an hour to get there and another thirty minutes to get the boat and gear out of the water and loaded up. We know that tomorrow will be another set day, and the forecast is for another winter storm. We'll be in it, getting ready for one more data point to use for science and to help conserve and manage the rivers. But, for now, we are living life in the present tense. We don't think too much about tomorrow. Ahead is a two-hour drive home and another hour to service the boat and the truck and to get everything ready for tomorrow.

It is then that we look at each other and, with unspoken acknowledgement, confirm that this day was good . . . the mission accomplished. We'd run our nets without losing any of them, there were fish caught, nothing broke . . . and the day produced no widows and no orphans. We are sailors "home from the sea" one more time. As river fisheries biologists we cannot ask for more.

Beyond the Twilight Zone

"Sssh! Turn off your light! Listen!" The sense of urgency in the words left no doubt that I should heed the instructions of the man in the mud beside me. I quickly clicked the switch to the off position on my light and grew very still. The two of us sat at arm's distance apart in the damp chill, enveloped by absolute darkness. I opened and shut my eyes. There was no difference—just black, complete black, overpowering black. I tried to control my breathing. The sound of it was absurdly loud. Then I faintly heard dripping water . . . drip . . . drip . . . drip . . . at regular intervals of a couple of seconds. The more I listened, the more my ears focused on it, the more pronounced the sound of the dripping became. Then, after about a minute, a coarse whisper crawled through the impenetrable darkness.

"Don't *you love* it?!"

I jumped. "Jesus Christ save me! Larry! You're crazy!"

Larry Willis and I were deep down in the earth on a mission. We were both graduate students at the University of Arkansas, employed by the university's zoology department to find and explore caves in southwestern Missouri and northwestern Arkansas. Larry was an experienced spelunker. I was employed to drag him from danger or share his fate. The object of our endeavors was to determine the whereabouts of a little white fish with no eyes, the Ozark cavefish, *Amblyopsis rosae,* a fish that grows to a maximum size of about two inches long and only lives in underground streams and pools. They lay an egg or two every couple of years and when they are lucky might catch and eat a cave cricket once or twice a year. That's it. There aren't very many of these little fish in the world. In fact, the only area where they were reported to exist was in a little pocket of limestone hills straddling the Arkansas-Missouri border. If we found any fish (a doubtful thing), we were to report our find via the university to the US Fish and Wildlife Service. The federal government would take it from there, potentially designating locations as critical habitat and perhaps even establishing a new national wildlife refuge. It was an adventurous way for a couple of college students to earn summer wages.

Most people have a certain fascination about caves. Perhaps it is because as a species we once lived in them. And if you think about it, we actually still live in caves. There weren't enough natural ones in the world for all of us so we started building "caves" out of sticks and mud. The further north you go in the United States, the more we use sticks. The further south you go, the more we use mud. The pattern probably has a lot to do with climate and the availability of clay (for bricks). Being the social critters that we are, we humans tend to build our caves in colonies . . . sort of like mud dauber wasps do.

Caves are the subject of science and adventuring. Many are quite beautiful, and for some, their beauty has been their curse. They have been trashed. Their walls have been covered with smoke (from torches), people's names, messages, and graffiti. Their formations have been broken, soiled, tromped down, or taken as souvenirs. Some have been commercialized to the point of absurdity, their interiors adorned by colored lights, their quiet periodically assaulted by music and raucous, ribald chatter. Some have been sealed, to protect life outside but dooming life within. Some, fortunately, have received protection. A few have been recognized as treasures and developed as features for parks sensitive to their fragility. In this last sense, only recently have we begun to recognize the interconnectedness of caves with environments and conditions up on the surface of the earth.

Caves come in many flavors. Some are dry and some are wet. The wet ones are considered to be "living caves" because they are in the process of forming. The dry caves bear testimony to a dynamic, changing world at mind-boggling temporal scales, a world subject to shifts of climate and geology over millions of years. The water comes for millions of years. Then for millions of years the water goes away. Caves can alternate between wet and dry. Yet situated as they are, deep in the earth, caves seem to have a timeless quality . . . at least it seems so from a human perspective. If we insert an evolutionary perspective into the mix, they are perhaps some of the more stable, unchanging environments on earth. There is no wind. The temperature is essentially constant and reflects the average annual temperature of the region. There are no seasons. Gravity and water, coupled with absolute darkness and quiet, are the only physical forces interfacing with life. Drip . . . drip . . . drip . . .

Our little cave fish has been in the Ozarks for a very long time. It evolved over tens of thousands if not millions of years from fish that swam upstream and into cave entrances. The entrances have to be pretty special. They have to have twilight zones—zones of transition—so that during the evolutionary process the fish could swim back out of the cave at will. There are still some species of schizophrenic fish (e.g., sculpins, *Cottus* spp.) frequently found in the twilight zones of Ozark caves, trying to decide what sort of fish they want to become . . . to be or not to be a "cave" fish.

The cave environment provided protection and stability for the precursor of the Ozark cave fish. The world of light provided the sun's energy necessary to produce things to eat. Little by little the fish changed. Little by little they moved ever deeper into the cave environment. They were, however, not the only things changing and finding caves to their liking. A group of small mammals developed the ability to find their way in the dark and to find food in the dark by chirping and listening for the echoes from the chirps. The skin between their fingers became webs. Over thousands if not millions of generations, the fingers grew longer and the webs filled the spaces. When the little mammals fell from high places, their fall was cushioned by the webs serving as built-in parachutes. In time, the little mammals learned how to move their arms in ways that not only arrested their fall but allowed them to actually gain altitude. They became bats. And it is bats that are responsible, ultimately, for the evolution of the little white fish in the caves.

The bats sleep and hibernate in caves, but they go outside of caves to find things to eat. When they've eaten, they return to the caves. Some bats are solitary, but many species are colonial. They like to cluster together when they rest in the caves. Below the places where they rest, deposits of bat feces develop. These "piles of poop" are the source of energy for life in the cave. The poop is colonized by fungi and bacteria that convert the stuff into a form usable by invertebrates like cave crickets, some species of little flies whose larvae hang on silk-like threads, a few spiders, and sowbugs (a kind of crustacean, like a "roly-poly" you find under boards). There typically aren't very many of these critters, but enough to keep biological energy flowing in the system. And all of that energy originates from outside of the cave. Without bats, life in the cave dies. The connections are pretty straightforward.

Larry and I were, however, connecting with caves through different pathways. We had to do it through social networking. The first order of business was simply to find out where caves in the region were located and then develop trust relationships with people who owned or controlled access to the caves. We developed a formula, a process for doing this. It worked beautifully. We let people discover us.

We were careful. We were quiet. We tried to project respect for the region's culture of independence and privacy. We knew and spoke the region's vernacular. We did not advertize our employer (the university). We used Larry's pickup truck rather than a government vehicle. We entered communities clean, well-groomed, armed with maps, a willingness to drink lots of coffee (or iced tea, depending on time of day), and an equal willingness to talk, if anybody wanted to talk . . . which they ultimately did.

Every little community has its gathering place. It's usually some small café or restaurant. They're pretty easy to find. All you have to do is drive through the community until you spot a bunch of pickup trucks parked out front. Once you park and walk inside, there is usually a table or booth where the local community leaders are gathered around mugs of coffee. Some will be eating breakfast, but most will be sipping coffee and talking.

We made a point of sitting a couple of tables or booths away from these groups . . . far enough away to avoid crowding their space but close enough that we'd be noticed. We'd order coffee, and sometimes breakfast, and then pull out our maps. This aroused little or no interest. There are always tourists passing through Ozark communities. They are seasonally important to local economies and thus are generally treated well, especially by business proprietors and waiters, but otherwise they are pretty much left alone. Once we got to our second cups of coffee, we'd shift seating and sit beside each other, making sure that we were facing the "power" table, spreading our maps in front of us, and conveniently leaving the seats in front of us free and open.

As natives of the Ozarks, Larry and I both had strong "twangs" in our speech. These twangs are the product of generations of conversing across the hollows between the hills ("hollars"). They can carry conversations across spaces without the need to be very loud. We could "holler" across the "hollar" and not be obtrusive.

We'd rustle the maps a little and project the word "cave" a few times, then pull out small pocket-sized notebooks and start scribbling. That generally was enough to stir the water at the power table. Usually it only took five or ten minutes at most before one or two ambassadors from the table would get up and come over to see what we were about.

"Where're you boys from?"

"Down in Arkansas."

"What're y'all doing?"

"Looking for blind fish in caves."

"How come?"

"Just try'n ta find out if there's any left."

If the ambassadors sat down in front of us, we were in business. If they called somebody else over from the power table, we were in gold. If extra chairs pulled up around us, we were in platinum.

People like to talk about caves. We'd introduce ourselves and then just settle back and let them talk. The tales could get pretty wild and sometimes pretty funny. There was always a tale about a bobcat or something else that could bite. Sometimes there was history . . . stories about the caves being used as hideouts by bandits or during the Civil War. After a while, following more coffee all around, somebody would generally figure out that we were OK, get nods all around, and say something like, "I've got a cave on my place. There's water in it but it don't come out the hole. Ain't no spring. Not sure where it [the water] goes. It's got spring lizards [salamanders] in it and white crawdads too [bingo!]. I used to crawl back in it years ago, but nobody goes there anymore. I don't let 'um. Got trapped in it once on a high spot when it flooded after a rain. Sort of cured me of the itch. Thought I was a goner. I can show you where it's at if you'd like. It's hard to find if you don't know where to look. The opening's covered up with bushes. Y'all got good lights?"

Within minutes and following handshakes all around and admonitions of "Y'all be careful now," we'd be in our truck following the cave's owner out into the country. Once we got on site, we'd start pulling our gear out of the back of Larry's truck, piece by piece. We knew that the cave's owner would be curious, and we wanted to seal our good relations by taking time to show him the equipment we had and what we used it for. It wasn't a process that could be rushed. And, in fact, it was good discipline for us too. It made us look at our stuff carefully and make sure that everything was there and in proper working condition.

Once we were suited up and ready to go, the cave's owner would usually stay with us until we crawled into the cave. If the entrance was large, sometimes he'd go with us for a while. But generally he'd say good-bye and head back to his truck.

We had to be really careful as we entered the caves, particularly the ones with small entrances, because more times than not, there'd be a snake there and we'd be on our bellies crawling. We didn't worry about cottonmouths, and there really weren't many rattlesnakes in the region, but copperheads were extremely common. Our work was during the summer, and by the time we got done at the café and got set to work, it would be midday and already hot. Snakes would be looking for, and usually already in, shady, cool spots where they would hang out until things cooled off a bit later in the day. Once past the entrance, however, the snake worries subsided. The snakes usually don't go very far inside.

Every cave was different. Sometimes the owner remembered something about them but just as frequently, memory had faded. Distances, long and short, were rarely correct. Sometimes the cave opened up quickly and allowed us to stand, at least a little. Other times the crawls could be really long. We wore helmets to keep from bumping our heads, but the rest of us got pretty banged up. Caves don't "give" much. That, for me, was actually a blessing. Being subject to claustrophobia, I didn't *want* them to give. I wanted those ceilings, those floors, and those walls to be strong and solid. Sometimes, when we got into large rooms, we'd find where parts of the ceiling had collapsed. There'd be rock rubble all over the floor of the cave. But, when we found this, we were usually relieved. When ceilings do that, they actually get stronger because it's usually the center that falls and the outside edges stay put. This creates a natural interior dome—one of the strongest of all architectural structures.

Some of the caves were old, relatively dry, and with few structures. But most of the caves we explored were beautiful inside. There'd be stalactites, stalagmites, flowstone, and curtains. For the most part they would be brown on the outside, but occasionally they'd sparkle like jewels. Some would go all the way from the ceiling to the floor. There would be drops of water on the tips of stalactites and stalagmites and general dampness on other features.

There would often be rim pools in the wetter caves, little pockets of water surrounded by small rock edges that had built up over time.

We'd push further and deeper into the caves, looking for water that could support cave fish. Sometimes it would be right there alongside of us in the main passageways. But just as often it would be down below us on some lower passageway. These were sort of scary. They meant that the floor we were on was a false floor that might crumble under our weight. We moved carefully, deliberately.

We found rivers in the caves and also large pools that somehow were connected to other water. We could tell when there were these connections because there'd be life in the pools. It might be a small aquatic crustacean, occasionally a white cave crayfish, and rarely (and to our delight) a cave fish. But we had to look hard to find these critters. In almost all cases they were solitary encounters in quiet pools.

Aquatic cave critters, especially cave fish, don't hang out in places with much, if any, current. It interferes with their ability to locate food, such as it might be. A cave fish doesn't have eyes, but its entire body is covered by special sensory structures that are used to feel small disturbances in the water (like when a bug falls in and wriggles). Cave fish also have very keen olfactory senses; they can track other aquatic critters along the bottom like a fine hunting dog on the trail of its game.

When we'd encounter a likely pool, Larry and I would spend a long time looking it over very carefully. The water would be very clear, but even so our lights would only penetrate two to three feet. Some of the pools were much deeper than that. If fish were in that deep water, we couldn't see them. But we understood, at least to some extent, cave fish biology and behavior. We'd put a finger into the water and move it on the surface to make a small disturbance, mimicking a bug in the water. If there were cave fish within a reasonable distance from that finger, up to around fifty to sixty feet, we'd see them slowly moving out from wherever they'd been, coming to investigate. At least half of the fish we saw during our study were revealed using this technique.

When I say "slowly" I really mean it. A cave fish is never in a hurry. It can't afford to be in a hurry. It takes energy to move. Using that energy is a critical investment for a fish that may only get to eat once or twice a year. Every movement has to be deliberate and well calculated. Return for investment is paramount.

Because of their rarity, we were not allowed to capture or even touch the fish that we encountered. Of course, nobody was watching, but we were governed by professional ethics. We also had to assume that the fish that we saw were indeed the species we were interested in. There are other species of cave fish, but according to the records, none of those other species were supposed to be in the region where we were working. The best we could do was occasionally to take a picture of a fish that was very close in very shallow water. Sometimes the photographs worked, but more often they did not work. There would be reflections from the water surface from the camera's flash that would spoil the shot. And we had to know our cameras very well. The absolute darkness surrounding us (our lights didn't matter) precluded use of any automatic features on the cameras. We had to match the aperture F-stop with shutter speed and know their synergistic appropriateness at different distances. As a result, the primary evidence of the fish we encountered would be the records that we kept in our notebooks. We'd have to estimate their size without having any reference for comparison. As scientists, we had to negotiate that piece of data between the two of us. It made a real difference because the presence of fish smaller than a certain size meant that we probably had a viable, reproducing population. Nobody really knew, however, how long a cave fish can live or how long it takes them to mature or even how to age the fish. The entire program was founded on assumptions and speculation . . . tough realms for scientists who by definition are supposed to base their work on count or measurement data. Even working within the framework of "presence and absence" was problematic. We could never be sure that we saw all the fish that were in a location or even that not seeing any fish meant that there were no fish there. Eventually we had to make peace with ourselves, knowing that we were doing the best that could be done. Not doing the work wasn't an option. The fate of the little cave fish was, essentially, in our hands. At least that was the premise upon which we founded our work. We did the best that we could, day after day, cave after cave, until finally we stopped at forty caves. Our total from those forty caves was eight fish . . . just eight fish . . . and six of them were from one cave.

The people Larry and I met during our explorations were careful with their land and generally very protective of their caves. When we'd come out of the caves more times than not the owner would be there at the cave's entrance, waiting on us. They wanted to know what we'd seen. Even more importantly, they wanted to know what we thought and felt about their caves. Most had close connections with their land, spiritually as well as physically and economically, were students of nature, and knew what sort of things lived on their property and in the caves. They wanted to know how caves worked. Many had tracked changes over time. Some expressed real concern about changes they'd seen in their lifetimes and wanted to know the best way to protect the caves. We did our best to provide information and perspective.

Was our work that summer worth the effort? Was it worth the expense? Was it worth the danger? You bet! When the US Fish and Wildlife Service received our report, they immediately began the process of purchasing the property and the cave where we'd found those six fish. It is now a designated national wildlife refuge.

But that designation is not enough to ensure the future of the Ozark cave fish. Not by a long shot. As we'd explain to the cave owners, the future of this very rare fish really resides up on top, where there is light. All of the parts of the world that make a cave ecosystem work have to be taken care of. The water in the cave comes from the surface somewhere. It has to be clean and free of contaminants. The insects that feed the bats out across the countryside have to be there for the bats to eat. Insecticides can tip the scale against the bats. If there aren't enough of the right kind of insects, there won't be enough bats to make enough deposits in the caves to feed the cave invertebrates that feed the cave fish. Additionally, if the bats are disturbed, especially during winter (which is a fine time to go cave exploring, plus there are fewer snakes around the cave entrances), they may wake up, start to fly, find little or nothing to eat (flying insects are typically not common during winter), pass critical energy thresholds, and starve. Bats are also very susceptible to disease because so many of them are colonial. If one bat gets sick, others soon follow. Entire colonies can be quickly wiped out. People who explore caves tend to wear the same old clothes, cave after cave. In doing so, they can spread disease among bat colonies.

So, what's the message here? Well, first of all there's the matter of understanding the interconnectedness that exists within and among the different ecosystems on earth. Everything is linked. When we lose parts of the whole, the whole has to do a reshuffle in order to keep on going. We don't really know, and might never know (until perhaps it is too late), what it takes to make the reshuffling something that's impossible to do. Second, we need to get past the thought of "What good is it?" Utility doesn't always have to equate with value. A cave does not really need to be commercialized in order to be valuable. Critters don't necessarily need to taste good to be considered important natural resources. Sometimes just "being" is enough value. That's somewhat easier to accept when the critter is something like a mockingbird that fills our days with song. But what about rare little fish, bats, and bugs down deep in the earth . . . in places where most of us don't, won't, or can't go? Do they matter? I really can't answer that question for anybody other than myself.

But here's something that is to me pretty sobering. This planet is the only place we've got to live. The more I engage science professionally and otherwise, the more I realize that I don't understand very much about the way life on this planet gets along. I increasingly feel like a water strider just scampering up on the surface of things. I have not and can not go very deep into the mechanism of things . . . as hard as I try. In fact, the deeper I try to go, the deeper the whole thing gets. At what point does it all fall apart.

God might care about us, and as a man of faith I believe that He does. But as a scientist, an ecologist, and a manager of natural resources, I can assure you that nature doesn't care at all. Little blind fish down in the earth might be there for a reason. If they go, what is the message from earth? What is nature's message? Are we smart enough . . . wise enough . . . to listen?

Woodland Pond

OPERATIONAL REALITY IS A MATTER OF SCALE. NOW, THAT'S THE sort of statement that just about any college or seminary professor can build a lecture around and in some cases an entire course. It doesn't matter really what the specific topic might be. Eyes will glaze over and there may be a sigh or two from the ranks of the semi-attentive (the rest of the class is already asleep). The time of day doesn't matter.

There can be exceptions, however. If you happen to be a professor of wildlife and fisheries, you can toss a bomb into the lecture hall by immediately following that opening statement with this: "Consider, for example, old ponds, sloughs, and hollows tucked back in the woods." Immediately, every duck hunter, eccentric angler, and woods crafter in the room will be brought to attention. Some will have panic written all over their faces because they are wondering if, during your ramblings, you've found *their* treasures. Others are hoping that a secret will be revealed.

Don't misunderstand. I love the sweep of mountain ranges and deserts. I am moved spiritually by the vastness of arctic taiga and tundra and by the open sea. As a river fisheries biologist, I teach and preach the importance of interconnectedness within landscapes and entire ecosystems.

But for as long as I can remember, there has been a special place in my heart for little hidden pockets of the wild. I am particularly drawn to woodland ponds. Life seems to ooze around and from them. And during the duck season the one on my farm is the foundation upon which almost every day rests. It tends to go completely dry during summer and, depending on autumn and winter rainfall, there are some years when it doesn't get water until after the duck season is over. But most years there's water in it during the season, and when there's water, there are ducks . . . not a lot, mind you, but enough to keep me charged with a hunter's spirit.

I could go to other places, bigger places, places with more ducks. I have keys to lots of gates and also annually lease a very large area that can at times have fabulous duck shooting. And yet my little woodland pond is like a siren calling . . . and it draws me back to it morning after morning.

It's on the back side of my farm, about a ten-minute walk from the gate where I park my truck. If the weather has been dry or if it is very cold and the ground is frozen, I could drive to it. But I don't do that. There's something about the walk from the gate to the pond that helps me transition into a hunter's mindset. As I walk to the pond I look at the stars and at the dark shadows of trees that are around the perimeters of my pastures. I listen to the owls and to the flights of geese passing overhead. Sometimes there's a coyote chorus, and if the weather has been warm and wet, early-breeding leopard frogs call. If there is frost, I enjoy hearing the crunch under my boots and seeing the sparkle from starlight.

My woodland pond is tucked down below my larger "fishing" pond. I sometime hunt ducks on that larger pond. If I do, there's opportunity for big ducks . . . mallards, gadwalls, widgeon, and an assortment of divers like ringnecks and scaup. But primarily my focus is on wood ducks. Wood ducks will also come to the larger pond, but their preference is that woodland pond. We seem to share values associated with time and place.

I groom that woodland pond when it's dry, picking up tree branches that may have fallen into it and stacking them to one side (so that I won't trip on them while hunting), trimming buttonbush limbs and sprouts to maintain a shooting hole, but leaving a big patch on the far end so that the ducks will have a safe roost at night . . . thick enough to keep the owls away. When full, the pond becomes chest deep out in the middle but most of it is thigh to waist deep . . . perfect for duck hunting.

When I arrive for a morning's hunt, I try to position myself in a way that keeps me in the shadows, with my back to the east. The shooting will be close, between fifty and seventy-five feet, so I use an open choke on my shotgun. Wood ducks are not large ducks, so I use small shot, usually number 4 steel. Because shots at wood ducks coming to my pond will be fast, I prefer to use a double-barrel shotgun with short barrels. My old pump gun is more rugged and has been a reliable partner for over forty years, but it is really better suited for the more open shooting that I get out on the larger pond. The double gun is lightning fast, and that's important for wood duck shooting.

Wood ducks coming into a woodland pond will generally give you warning as they approach. The hens will call and squeal when they are nearing the spot they intend to land in. But the warning really doesn't help the shooter. When the ducks drop in through the tree branches they twist, turn, bob, and weave in absolutely unpredictable ways. Shooting wood ducks in this sort of situation is and must be absolutely instinctive. They typically give no opportunity for deliberate shooting. They are suddenly just there, all around you, in a flurry of wings and splashes. If they get on the water before you can shoot, they will quickly look around to make sure all is well. If you move (which you should) they will almost immediately flush. Once airborne again, they'll hug the shadows and then twist away through the trees. Their navigational skills and ability to see things in the low light of early morning and at top speed are absolutely amazing. Unless you shoot quickly, they'll be gone and you'll be duckless. Even if you do shoot, odds are that you will still be duckless. They are a tough target and I love them for it.

As I take my position on the pond, I complete my transition from the other world to the world of a hunter. A different realm of being envelopes me and touches both mind and heart. I watch the sky as it turns from blue black to gray. Sometimes I can hear the whistle of wings as early flocks of ducks pass high overhead on their way to distant feeding areas. Most mornings I have a couple gray squirrels in the trees around me, slipping as ghosts along the branches of trees lining the pond, following an arboreal highway known only to them. As the sky lightens, there will almost invariably be a woodcock that will fly over the pond. I know this will usually happen, but in spite of myself, when that woodcock comes over, I instinctively raise my gun, thinking at first that it is a wood duck coming to the pond. The woodcock is my timer. Once the woodcock has passed, there likely will be wood ducks within five minutes. My gun needs to be loaded when the woodcock passes.

It is a rare day when at least one or two little bunches of ducks don't come to my woodland pond. But every morning I still have that wonderful sense of uncertainty that is so important to a hunter. I strain to hear the call of incoming ducks. And then, all of a sudden, the call is there. Sometimes it happens far enough in advance that I can shuffle my feet and get ready. More often, however, it happens just moments before the ducks come twisting and turning down through the opening in the treetops.

If I'm on my game, I'll drop one and sometimes even two ducks as they come in. If they are shot fairly high over the water, they will hit the water with a hard smack. If lower, the impact will be more of a soft splash. Regardless, when shot ducks are on the water you have to be prepared to anchor them. Wounded wood ducks can quickly get their bearings and escape. A retriever, if you have one (and I have), is priceless.

If the ducks are moving well, shooting a two to three duck limit can happen quickly. By the time the sun rises, thirty minutes into the hunt, most wood ducks are already where they want to be for the morning and the shooting essentially stops. Subsequently, it is a good idea to leave the pond as soon as you have your ducks for the day, whether it's one duck or the limit. That way, you're gone if fresh ducks start working the area, and, hopefully, those fresh ducks that arrive later will come back to the pond the next day.

But there's an entirely different aspect to the pond and to these hunts. Although I am a hunter and I certainly do shoot, the older I get, the less the shooting matters. Early morning wood duck hunts on the woodland pond serve a greater purpose for me now than providing the basic ingredients for a duck dinner. And they have been doing so for quite a while. They are instrumental in moving me into a spiritual realm . . . with the pond and the dawning of new day combining to become a sanctuary for disciplined, focused prayer. These hunts have, in fact, become my winter sacraments. They are the conduits of connectivity, the means for discernment and enlightenment, the lights along pathways to the oversoul, and an important source of wind to fill the sails of a mortal's sojourns into faith.

I tend to pray alone. Subsequently, I tend to be a solitary wood duck hunter. The solitude makes a difference. In some ways it is like fasting. Solitary hunts help me focus and make peace with unanswered and unanswerable questions. When I am alone, away from the inevitable talk that comes when duck hunting with companions, the quiet and serene beauty of dawn instills in me a sense of meaning that transcends understanding. It is not something that words can express. My reflections while standing in the shadows of a tree, waiting for the ducks to arrive, help clarify purpose and relationships among all sorts of things. The rush of adrenaline following arrival of the ducks, along with the shooting, compels me to express thanksgiving for living in a place where I can go hunting and have and shoot a gun, for wood ducks and the wild that they represent, and ultimately for all the treasures that are a woodland pond.

In this final regard, the woodland pond on my farm long ago transitioned in my heart and in my mind from being something "out there" and separate from me into something that has essentially enveloped me. With time I came to realize that although I may have legal title to the land and the pond, I do not, I *cannot* possess it because I am actually part of it. We are inextricably combined one with the other.

I'd sensed that this was happening after only a few years of interacting with the pond. But I was determined not to let it happen. I worked hard to control my heart in order to avoid establishing deep connections with the pond. I had plans to move on to somewhere else following retirement. I didn't want to love "my" land and "my" pond. Love would make it too hard to sell, too hard to leave. So I enjoyed the pond and all that it provided, but I kept a spiritual distance from it. Its purpose was solely utilitarian . . . but in a beautiful sort of way. There would be no sense of attachment. I would take care of the place and nurture it in accordance with my profession in natural resources management. Then, if situations developed appropriately, I could sell the place and move on. But love it? Absolutely not! I was dead set against letting that happen.

Well, I should have known better. I should have realized from the beginning that I wasn't really in charge of the affair. I may be the captain of the ship, but I am certainly not the wind in the sails.

Since childhood I'd prayed that somehow, someway, in my life, I would be totally, completely, comprehensively melded with the spirits and rhythms of the earth in some wild place. The prayers continued unabated across the decades. They stimulated wild imaginings, restlessness, and discontent. But I continued praying, with my thoughts wrapped around visions of it all happening in some remote region of mountains, tundra, tropical jungle, or perhaps even desert. I never imagined that my prayers would be answered as they were . . . that God would link with me so powerfully through a brushy little pond tucked back in a quiet corner of the woods on a Mississippi farm. But that's exactly what happened, in spite of my efforts to live in a state of association but not in a state of love.

As I reflect deeper on the entire situation, it dawns on me that the little woodland pond out there on the farm has probably been responsible over the years for saving my career, my marriage, my sanity, and perhaps even my life. If that pond and all that it has brought into my life had not existed . . . well . . . the thought of it not being there makes me shutter.

Operational reality is a matter of scale. When it comes to applying this concept to little woodland ponds, I am, as a scientist, faced with a fundamental challenge: humankind has not yet figured a way to measure spirit. But I do know this: the spiritual power emanating from that pond is all out of proportion to its size. Perhaps I need to measure influence rather than the thing itself. Physicists do this, so why not naturalists who base much of their work on the foundations of science. All I'd have to do is figure out a way to measure joy, peace, satisfaction, excitement, and love (among others). On the other hand, perhaps it just might be better to graciously accept blessings, acknowledge their source, and move ahead on the mortal pilgrimage . . . with visions of sunrises filled with whistling wings. Must we ask "Why?" or "How?" when we're given a gift? Maybe the proper response is simply to return the love.

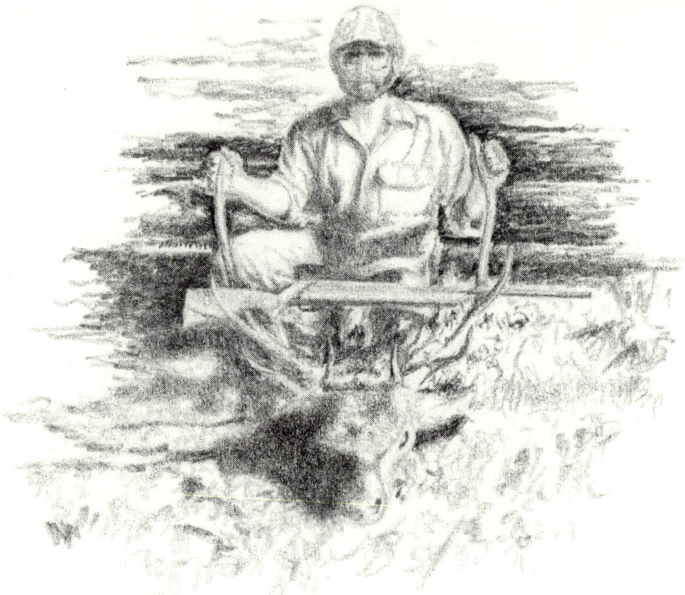

Sagebrush Bull

Whispering to each other, hardly daring to move from beyond the boulder's shadow where we lay, my hunting companion, Randy Robinette, and I could hardly believe the scene unfolding across the valley. A gentle wind riffled the grass near us. A pair of mallards coasted into a marshy beaver pond. Shadows from occasional clouds played on the mountain slopes. Slowly, stately, deliberately, a herd of elk filtered out of dark timber and into the open of a sagebrush meadow. The drama before us held us spellbound. Scarcely an hour had passed since we'd left our cabin to scout for elk. The next day would be opening day of the Colorado elk season and we'd stumbled into a hunter's paradise.

Suddenly a bull in the herd sent his eerie flute-like primeval call drifting through the mountains. Its echoes lingered for several moments on air that had suddenly grown incredibly still. We were transfixed by the absolute wildness of that bull elk's call. Our whispers ceased. The bull's call touched some fiber within me, creating an ancient longing that permeated throughout my entire body, causing me to shiver. I knew that I was where I was supposed to be . . . a hunter responding to his own primeval calling that reverberated from the depths of his soul and merged with the call from the bull.

A month earlier, had someone ventured to suggest that I'd be in Colorado with exclusive rights to hunt what may be some of the finest elk range in the country, I'd have shrugged off the comment, turned back to my desk, and continued with my work. For me, elk hunting was hardly even a dream. The possibilities of engagement were simply too remote.

Elk range is restricted, for all practical purposes, to the western regions of North America. It requires access to a lot of country and, in many instances, the services of a professional guide . . . particularly if you want a crack at a decent bull. Aside from the well-worn trails of some public lands, I knew of no place to go. And, as far as guides go, they were far beyond any price range affordable by me as a young assistant professor. Then Randy came knocking at my office door and informed me that we had an invitation to hunt on a thousand-acre ranch in Colorado that was owned by the family of one of his graduate students. Realizing the potential, I jumped on that offer. Now, here we were, on the side of a mountain, watching what had been a dream of mine for nearly a lifetime take shape in front of us.

We watched that herd of elk for the better part of an hour as they moved up the valley. Then, as shadows deepened in the final minutes of the day, they faded back into the dark timber. Slowly we stood, stretched, looked at each other as only hunters can do when they sense the dawning of adventure, collected ourselves and our thoughts, and quietly started making our way back along a dusty ranch road to the cabin that would be our hub for the week's hunt.

The road back to the cabin led through a small patch of timber, and while passing through the timber in the dusky light of late evening, another herd of elk thundered down upon us, bodies heaving, hooves pounding, nostrils flared, and billowing steam in the chilled mountain air. They suddenly sensed our presence and came to an abrupt halt all around us. Some were so close that I could see a glint of moonlight on their eyes. Then they rushed on down the mountainside, leaving us awestruck with their magnificence and wildness.

The following morning Randy and I slipped quietly out of the old ranch cabin and started a cautious climb up to the ridge where we been the previous evening and that would give us, as dawn drifted on the landscape, a commanding view of practically the entire valley. Our footsteps were muffled by thick dust on the ranch road. A coyote yelped. A couple of ducks passed overhead on whispering wings. Even in the darkness we could see that the dust in the road was covered with tracks. However, on close inspection, most of the tracks turned out to be those of mule deer, not elk. Randy had a mule deer tag, but I didn't. My focus was elk and I was determined not to drift.

We finally arrived at our vantage point on the ridge. In the predawn light we could see the valley with the beaver pond, stands of dark timber across the valley, and scattered sagebrush meadows. Another narrow ranch road that we hadn't seen the previous evening snaked its way along the base of the mountain. There also was the ruin of a long-abandoned cabin tucked away near a jumble of rocks. After wishing each other good luck, we split up. Randy would hunt the upper part of the valley. I'd hunt the lower sections.

I watched Randy fade into the predawn darkness and then stood for several minutes looking across the expanse of the valley before me. The mountains were barely outlined as the first hint of dawn lightened the sky. The odor of sagebrush filled the air. During those minutes I did not move, trying to capture the essence of a Rocky Mountain morning.

For me the southern Rockies are full of majesty but the sense of wilderness in them isn't strong. Wild . . . yes, but wilderness . . . not really. There are certainly wild areas, but even the wildest seem to have felt the touch of humankind. Roads and fences are constant reminders that this is country long settled. But just as in the wild places of the southeastern United States, a hunter can still find the spirit of the land, *if* the hunter will take the time to listen to its rhythms . . . and connect with them.

Regardless, it was good to be among mountains again . . . to breathe crisp, cool, dry air and to shoulder my scratched and worn rifle. I'd been away from mountains for a couple of years since joining the faculty at Mississippi State University. I'd moved to Mississippi from Alaska and, frankly, the transition had been challenging. Alaska had wilderness and mountains, entire ranges of them . . . ranges that had surrounded me with their magnificence. I missed mountains. I missed vistas. I missed being able to stretch my eyeballs. I missed the sweep of valleys. My formative years in the Ozarks, coupled with my time in Alaska, treks in Nepal, and excursions in the mountains of Australia, Southeast Asia, Africa, and Central America had imprinted mountains in my soul. I couldn't imagine living my life where there were no mountains, but I was doing it in Mississippi. Now, here on this elk hunt in Colorado, I sensed a deep awakening. As I stood there alone, there in the dawning of a Rocky Mountain day, I felt synchrony with all that surrounded me . . . here in the land of Jim Bridger and Sam Bass . . . rambling and hunting in the domain of the "mountain men" of the late 1800s. I knew that I'd been born a hundred years too late, but better late than never, and happiness filled my heart. I was, absolutely, a happy man, in a place I really like, doing what I loved to do—hunt big game.

About fifteen minutes after Randy left me, with dawn flush on the horizon, I worked my way down through a jumble of rocks to a large boulder that I'd selected as the starting point for my morning's hunt. Not only would it give me a commanding view of the valley and mountains, it would break the crisp wind that had picked up since leaving the cabin and break up my outline as I scanned the valley for elk.

Less than ten minutes after settling down, a bull elk bugled in the upper reaches of the valley. This bull was in Randy's sector. I knew that after hearing that bull Randy would be hot on its trail. Silently I sent positive waves toward Randy, then focused my attention again on the lower valley that swept before me.

The light was strong enough now for me to see details in the valley. Then, far away, across the valley, at least a mile from me, two brown spots emerged from the edge of a sagebrush meadow. With my binoculars I confirmed that they were elk, but at that distance I couldn't tell if they were cows or bulls. Colorado game regulations specified that only bulls with at least four points on one antler could be taken.

Those elk not only were far way, they were also moving. I was going to have to hustle if I expected to intercept them before they drifted back into the forest. Once in the timber, they'd be virtually impossible to stalk. But, although moving steadily, they really didn't seem to be in a hurry to finish their breakfast out there in the sagebrush meadow. Maybe I had a chance . . .

Scrambling down from my rocky perch, I crossed the dusty road and then ducked down along the edge of an aspen grove. I'd gone perhaps a hundred yards or so when a big mule deer doe bounced up in front of me. She ran into a thicket and then turned to look me over. I just kept moving and she vanished into the aspens.

From the aspens I moved down along a creek bottom choked with alders. It was tough going and at times I was forced to crawl on my hands and knees. Finally I broke through to the opposite side and climbed to a vantage point to check on the elks' location.

They were still in the meadow and had been joined by several other elk. But they were still too far for me to see antlers. Then I heard a bull among them bugle and my heart skipped a beat. I was in business. There was a bull to stalk!

At this point I realized that the original route I'd selected wouldn't work. The elk had already moved beyond rifle range of the rocks I'd intended to use for my bushwhack. I was going to have to circle around a ravine, climb the side of a mountain up a steep cliff, and then try to cut them off higher up on the slopes.

I was tempered, however, with the realization that, if needed, I had an entire week of elk hunting ahead of me. I really didn't feel much pressure. It was, after all, the first hour of the first day of the season. If this stalk didn't work, there would be others. I was fairly confident about that. With that tempering, I settled down. I didn't want to rush the stalk but rather to quietly ease along the mountain, climbing ever higher until I reached the upper edge of the meadow. If things worked out, then great. If not, that was OK. But I would do my best. That was what this hunt was all about.

I scrambled across a beaver dam that spanned the creek coursing through the valley. Once across the creek, I started my climb. Slowly and deliberately I worked myself up the side of the mountain. The terrain was much steeper and much rockier than I'd anticipated. In order to gain elevation, I had to tack back and forth across stretches of loose rocks. I had to be very careful with those loose rocks. Not only were they a hazard to me as a climber, they also, if disturbed, would go tumbling down the mountain, alerting the elk to my presence.

Finally I made it to a small ridgeline. The sun was fully up by that time. The day was warming and I'd already begun to sweat. This alarmed me. I couldn't afford sweating because of the risk of my scent drifting to the elk. As the day warmed, there would be updrafts from the valley to the slopes and the elk. The elk knew this. That is why they were working the slopes in the way that they were. So I stopped for a few minutes and let the wind whip me until I was dry.

It only took about five minutes for me to cool down and get dry. In this regard, Colorado mountain air is a blessing for big game hunters! Then with a deep breath, I continued with my stalk. There was one final stand of dark timber that lay between me and the meadow where I'd last seen the elk. I entered the shadows of that timber and moved quietly along a game trail for about two hundred yards. There was a hush that enveloped me. The shadows were deep. The currents of my soul, a hunter's soul, were even deeper. I could feel the deep reverberations of primeval purpose and identity taking command. The drama might have been that of ten thousand years ago . . . and perhaps it was.

Suddenly, I sensed the presence of animals around me. I'm not sure exactly what it was that alerted me, but I knew that there were large animals nearby. I couldn't see them. I couldn't smell them. I had not heard anything. But I was sure that there was something close to me. My hunter's sense told me so. So I came to an abrupt halt and just stood where I was, next to a large spruce tree. I saw nothing. I heard nothing. But still I made no move. Then I heard a stick crack somewhere deep in the shadows of the ravine ahead of me. The air was so still. There was tension in that air . . . the sort of tension you feel just before a bolt of lightning strikes nearby. My senses came to full attention. My breathing slowed and my heart moved in cadence with that breathing. There was purity in the moment, the clean purity than purges the dust and clutter of a man's soul. Then . . . across the ravine . . . into a small meadow . . . a bull elk walked out from the shadows of aspens.

He was magnificent. His antlers flashed in the sun as he tossed his head. He was regal. He was beautiful in the most absolute sense of the word. Muscles rippled along his neck and shoulders. His dark neck stood out in sharp contrast to his smooth, tan-colored body, a body that towered about the sagebrush. He knew that he was the king, the master of his world. His every step confirmed this. And he was looking directly at me!

The bull was approximately 150 yards away. Although I was in the shadows of the timber, I was still caught out in the open between trees. I could not move. There was no way that I would be able to find a steady rest against a tree trunk or on a rock or stump and absolutely no way that I could drop to my knees for a steadier shot. Any move . . . any move at all . . . would send this bull crashing out of my life forever.

I had no choice but to take an offhand, standing shot. Slowly, I raised my rifle. As I did so, the bull riveted his attention on me. I knew that there were only precious fleeting moments until the drama would crest. Through the rifle's scope I could tell absolutely that his magnificent antlers met the legal criteria. Their sweep along his back, their flashing ivory-colored tines, their deep mahogany main beams left no doubt that this was the bull I'd dreamed about for years . . . since childhood. I dropped the crosshairs of the scope immediately to his chest, but then shifted my aim and held a little high.

I shoot an old Winchester .30-06 Model 70 bolt-action rifle. This caliber is pretty much of a minimum caliber for elk. I figured that a chest shot would kill him but that before he died he might cover a lot of ground. I didn't want to lose him in these mountains. So I held high. Either I'd break his back and put him on the ground immediately or I'd miss him completely and he'd escape unhurt.

All of these thoughts passed through me in the course of just a few seconds. That was all the time I had. Then I squeezed the trigger and eight hundred pounds of elk crashed to the ground. He wasn't dead, but he was definitely down. He struggled to his front feet, then collapsed again. I jacked a fresh round into my rifle but didn't have a chance for a second shot. The bull tumbled, thrashed, and then rolled back into the small stand of aspens from where he'd come. Gosh what a ruckus he made on that mountainside!

Suddenly, I was surrounded by elk. Cow elk were everywhere. I'd walked right into the middle of that bull's harem. They had been the source of that animal presence that I'd felt earlier, but I had not seen a single one of them. Now they rushed through the timber, across the meadow and the ravine, and up the side of the mountain. But my focus was on that bull. I kept my attention and my rifle aimed at where I'd last seen him. He was out of sight, but I knew where he'd gone down and etched the place, as in stone, in my mind.

I waited five minutes. All was quiet in the brush and on the mountainside. Only ravens broke the silence as I slowly, carefully, and silently worked my way down into the ravine and back up the other side to where the bull had stood when I'd shot. My plan was to approach from above the aspens where the bull had gone down.

Every step was deliberate. With each one, I would search the landscape before me to be certain that there wouldn't be a surprise encounter with that bull.

Once on the other side, I carefully checked the ground where the bull had been. There was blood and evidence of the bull's struggle all over the place. Then, suddenly, only thirty yards away, there was a crashing in the brush. The bull was trying to get to his feet again. Up he came! At this close range the reality of his awesome size momentarily shocked me. He was huge! His eyes were wide; there was blood on his side. Without hesitation I shot him through the shoulder and he went down again, this time for keeps. The smell of crushed vegetation mingled with that of burned gunpowder and the dank odor of a bull elk in rut. I reloaded my rifle again and walked slowly to the bull. I moved into position just below him and, standing no more than ten feet away, watched as he took his last breath. Then he was still. I had my elk . . . sort of . . .

Standing there by him, my first thoughts were focused on his size. Up until that moment my largest big game animal had been a mature black bear up in Alaska. This elk was more than twice the size of that bear and several times as large as deer I'd shot in the southeastern United States.

The antlers were more beautiful than I'd calculated through the rifle's scope prior to my shot. The tines were long, symmetrical, and highly polished. Each antler had four points. There are certainly larger elk, and elk with larger antlers, but this bull was for me a perfect trophy. He was a good bull, a decent bull. I felt good about him. I felt good about the stalk and about the shooting. But then reality sobered me. I was alone on the side of a mountain with a dead elk that weighed at least five times more than I did.

It is tempting to simply say that I processed the elk in the field and packed him down off the mountainside, and that it took two days to pull off this enterprise. That's the way most hunting stories go. But I'm not going to do that. I'm not going to "sugar coat" the part of the hunt that is typically not shared. I think that doing so would be an injustice not only to the hunt, but to hunters who, like me, understand the power of the generally unspoken chapters of their affairs. So here it goes. Take a deep breath. (I certainly did!)

Grabbing a hind leg, I tried to roll the bull over onto his back. Finally, with a heave, over he came; and then, to my horror, he started sliding down the mountainside! I was down slope from him and HERE HE CAME! My life flashed before me. I was about to be crushed by a dead elk! Kicking rocks, grabbing bushes, and scrambling as hard and fast as I could, I jumped and then dove and tumbled out of the way, landing in a jumble of boulders and skinning and cutting more parts of me than I care to relate. That elk roared past me in a mix of small rocks, dust, and sticks—snapping small saplings and sliding perhaps twenty feet down the mountain before his antlers became tangled in a clump of small alders, where he came once again to rest.

When the dust had settled he was still on his back, secured by trees and ready for field dressing. I was shaking all over. It had been a close call, much too close . . . the sort of freak event that nobody ever thinks about until it happens. "Crushed by a freshly killed elk sliding down the mountain . . ." I could almost read my obituary.

But now he was secure. I made sure of that with a bit of extra rope lashing between antlers and alder saplings. Then, whipping out my old Buck folding knife, I started to work, beginning my cut down between his hind legs, removing the testicles in order to prevent them from tainting the meat, then working my way up to where the chest meets the abdomen. I learned very quickly that elk hide is tough stuff. Finally, however, I got him opened up.

I was confronted at this point with around two hundred pounds of internal organs. With the elk on his back and securely wedged in the trees, I was going to have to somehow haul all of those organs from his body cavity. There would be none of this dainty business of tenderly rolling the animal to its side and letting gravity do its work, as is done with most deer. No sir. I had to deal with this bull elk as it was presented to me.

Steam rolled out of the freshly opened elk and fogged my glasses. Goodness gracious he was hot inside! It was essential that I get this beast cooled off before the meat started to spoil. I had to get the body cavity cleaned out and the hide off—pronto! So after pulling off my shirt, I reached deep into the slick mass, up to my shoulders, groping with one hand for something to grip, cutting mesentery with the other hand, and trying to hold onto a knife handle now made slippery in the wet morass. I didn't want to even think about losing my knife down inside that elk. Moving forward and ever deeper, I began working around the diaphragm that separated the abdominal cavity from the chest cavity. Once cleared, I reached forward as far as I could with both arms, severed the windpipe and large dorsal aorta with the hand holding the knife, and yanked with the other hand. Lungs and heart ripped loose, paving the way for eventual triumph.

An hour had passed . . .

I walked backward with one hand clutching the heart and lungs and the other tightly embracing the stomach and intestines, slowly, ripping and stretching, and the entire mass crept up out of the body cavity and slipped over the side! Victory!

Then I turned to the bull's rear end like a vulture and, with my knife, encircled the anus with a deep cut, freeing it from its attachment to the hide. I forced my hand through the cut and, reaching deep inside and gripping the outside of the colon, pulled backward as hard as I could. The gut broke free and came out along with the tag end of the large intestine that had remained in the body cavity. The opening created by this procedure provided the conduit through which blood trapped in the body cavity began to drain.

Another hour had passed . . .

I focused then on removing the cape and head. The skinning went fairly easy, but it took more than forty-five minutes to finally slice through the neck, separating the skull from the atlas vertebra. I pulled the head, antlers, and neck skin to one side and left them on a rock. I estimated that they weighed over fifty pounds.

By this time, Canada jays and magpies had gathered as a sort of cheering section, watching my work and coaching me. They were sneaky little beggars, bold and arrogant at times, waiting for me to drop my guard so that they could dart in and grab a bit of my elk. Like an old grizzly on his kill, I growled at them and swung at them with bloody paws. Cutting a stick, I tried to knock them off the carcass. They were relentless. We harassed one another off and on the rest of the morning. It wasn't until I threw a scrap of meat onto the gut pile that a truce of sorts was proclaimed.

By noon, I'd removed both front quarters, both hind quarters, and both back straps. These I hung in a tree to cool. I had them freely suspended twenty feet above the ground by a rope in order to keep bears from stealing them. All that remained were scraps and ribs. I could attend to these later upon my return . . . if they were still there. Then I wrapped the elk's antlers with my blaze orange hunting vest, bent low, grabbed the antlers, and swung head, antlers, and neck skin directly over my head and onto my shoulders. The elk's forehead rested perfectly on my shoulders just below my neck. The brow tines stuck out on either side of my face. I positioned my rifle across the second pair of tines, draped my arms across the rifle, and began my trek down the side of the mountain. My destination: cabin, some two or three miles away as the crow flies. But my path would be longer than that. There was no direct way off that mountain. I wasn't sure of anything except the general direction. I knew where I was. I knew the valley and the mountain. But I didn't know the best way to pack an elk off that mountain. My trek would be by guess and by gosh, following the lay of the land and game trails.

I took the first cautious step with my load, felt the balance, adjusted it, and felt that it was good. I took another step, then another . . . then there was rhythm . . . and then the rhythm caught me up and brought poetry and song back into the hunt and into my heart. On and on and on, down through the timber and across meadow after meadow, along ridges, through creeks, on and on and on . . . no compass, just the sun and the wind and the sage and the timber and the rocks and the sky and me.

My thoughts entered the timeless realms of the oversoul as I made my way down that mountainside with this, my first load of my first elk. Words swirled deep within me, only occasionally breaking free as whispers, words metered to match the rhythms of my trek down the mountain. They first came as prose but with the hours became song. I remember them so clearly . . .

Sagebrush bull
Flashing antlers in the sun
Lord, king of the meadows and timber
Power surging, proclaiming your reign,
Wilderness call penetrates—touching my soul.

Sagebrush bull
Magnificent incarnation of life
Magnificent even as you crashed to earth—
Echoes of my shot, thundering hooves, cries of ravens
Reverberate through these sacred mountains.

Sagebrush bull
You are mine
But, I was almost yours.
I am stilled by it all,
I am chilled by it all,
I am strengthened by it all—
Burned on mind, etched on heart
Power and spirit were transferred from you to me.

Sagebrush bull
Our destinies joined,
We are one
Mystical, mythical creature of dreamtime,
We've resurrected the ancient pageant of the age.

Sagebrush bull
I am carrying you to my camp.
To carry you makes me stronger,

I feel strong carrying you,
The strongest of my life—
I am a man in his prime
Just as you are a bull in your prime.
This day is ours,
We are blessed.

It took me a couple of hours to get down off that mountain with my load. When I got to the base of the mountain, at the edge of the valley, I intersected the ranch road that Randy and I had discovered earlier that morning. It seemed to lead in the general direction of camp. I followed it. An hour later, I was at our cabin.

There I left the elk's antlers and cape, along with a note to Randy, telling him where I was and what I was doing. I made a quick sandwich, put my rifle in its case, refilled my water bottle, and started back to where I cached the elk meat. But this time I had my good frame pack with me.

There was a song in my heart as I left the cabin, and it only got stronger as I made my way back through the valley and to the meat. There was no hurry. I had my elk and I had time to bring him to camp.

It did take me two days to get the elk packed in from the mountain and to the cabin. Fortunately, I had no bear problems. Once the meat was in camp, I shifted into a totally different realm of being. I became camp master, cutting and packaging meat, cooking, piddling (which I love!), working with knives, sharpening them, cleaning and oiling my rifle, tidying camp, and, later in the week, helping Randy haul his elk out of the upper reaches of the valley.

My journal from this hunt reads: "I like being 37 years old and able to do this sort of thing. I like very much the demands of being a big game hunter, sweating, heaving, wresting, heaving loads, jumping mule deer, listening to ravens, and thinking ahead to a supper of fresh elk steaks. Big sky, big country. It is a life that cannot be beat!"

I wrote those words nearly a quarter of a century ago, and they are still as valid as ever. And as I write *these* words, sitting here with gray beard and a body that struggles to keep its strength and endurance, I feel a surging within me . . .

Storm on the Kapuas

The dusty jeep turned off of the main road and onto a narrow lane through the village, navigating slowly to avoid bumps, chickens, and small groups of the faithful on their way to the mosque for evening prayers. It had been a long two-day overland journey from the Indonesian city of Pontianak through the Borneo countryside and on to the village where we would begin our work on the Kapuas River. Along the way we'd passed through small timber settlements and occasional farming communities, stopping occasionally for tea and meals and spending the night in the home of the jeep driver's uncle.

It was good to be back in Southeast Asia. On this particular assignment I was working for the US Agency for International Development (USAID), conducting assessments of river fisheries. Although centered in Java, my work was to focus primarily on Sumatra and Kalimantan (Borneo). I'd already finished my work in Sumatra, and now, after several weeks of emersion, working alone with Indonesians, my ability to speak Bahasa had come back in pretty good form. This needed to happen before I would be ready to work in remote Borneo.

Southeast Asia is my other world . . . one that captured me as a young man and has held tightly to me over the decades. When I'm there I'm a different man. The land, the people, the pace of life, the forests and mountains and rivers—all wrap themselves around my heart and fill it with beautiful energy. The music, the calls to prayer from mosques, the sweet calls of magpie robins and the liquid calls of orioles, the force of midday sun, the intensity of the afternoon rain, the whining of insects, the shadows in the jungle as day fades to night, the roadside cafés and the quiet way of the people are all in synchrony with who I am deep in my soul. I walk with a different pace when in Asia. I move through days in a different rhythm . . . I linger over meals and cool drinks.

The jeep's driver finally found the small hotel where we'd spend the night and pulled to a stop in front of it. I crawled out, stretched, slapped the dust from my pants, and reached for my bags. The Indonesian biologist, Agus, got his bags and joined me as I walked through the open door of the hotel and to the counter to check in.

"Pukul berapa kami akan pergi makan malam?" (What time are we going to have supper?), I asked.

"Lebih baik kalau kami pergi makan selepas symbaya" (It is best if we wait until after prayers), Agus replied.

"Baik, la. Rancangan itu memberi kepada saya cucup masa untuk mandi, tukar pakian, dan juga cari bir sejuk daripada kedai Cina disana" (Good. That plan gives me enough time to shower, change clothes, and also go find a cold beer at that Chinese shop over there).

Agus smiled. Being Muslim, he didn't drink beer, but he could appreciate the power of cold refreshment at the end of a hot day and the way it served as a catalyst to assist with the transition from day to evening to night in the tropics.

I got the key to my hotel room, grabbed my gear, and went up a creaky staircase to locate my room. The hotel was like so many in this part of the world. The rooms are clean but Spartan, with a bed, a lamp, a chair, and sometimes a small table or desk. On the ceiling was pasted an arrow pointing toward Mecca. The walls had old paint but it still hung on without peeling. There was a pair of plastic slippers to wear when going down the hallway to the communal *mandi* (shower). There was, however, a sink in the room, and a small towel and bar of soap. Near the window was a portable fan. House geckos crawled on the walls and the ceiling.

I slipped out of my clothes, wrapped myself in a sarong, slipped on the plastic slippers, and went down the hall for my mandi. The cool water felt good. There typically is no hot water in remote hotels of this sort. But who would want hot water? The whole idea is to knock off the dust and get refreshed.

Returning to my room, I dressed, put on my sandals, slipped my passport and money into a pigskin pouch, tucked the pouch under my shirt and down inside the front of my trousers, pulled the drawstring of the pouch tight around my waist, and walked out the door. As I got to the lower level I could see that the tiny community was already coming to life. Tables and chairs were being set up along the streets. Cooking carts of all sorts were being arranged and fires started. Music began to drift through the twilight. Swifts were making their last chittering forays before settling into their roosts. Geckos were chirping and darting after insects attracted by the lights inside the tea shops.

I prowled the streets for a while, then settled down at a table in front of the Chinese shop. The waitress came to me and spoke to me in Bahasa. People just assume that you speak Bahasa when you are this deep in the Indonesian countryside. It is sort of like sitting down in a café somewhere in Kansas. The language in Kansas is English. But in larger cities it is more common for Indonesians to speak to westerners in English rather than Bahasa. It was good to be beyond that cross-cultural interface, to be in the flow of deeper, purer Southeast Asian currents.

I ordered my beer and a plate of fried noodles, pulled out my journal, and began writing notes and thoughts from the day. There was magic in the twilight. The call to prayer drifted across the town, somehow purified and made more holy by passing through the last vestiges of a tropical sunset. My beer came, the bottle wet with condensation, and, as the cap was removed, a small cloud formed momentarily over its mouth. Taking a sip, I leaned back in my chair, the full-bodied flavor of Asian beer awakening taste buds that had been inactive and asleep for much too long. Then I took a long draw from the bottle and settled into my writing as the tropical night quickly settled over the land.

When in Asia, my journal is my constant companion. Within it are the tracks of my passing . . . with regard to not only the physical journey, but also those of the deeper sort. Asia draws me into a different realm of being, into introspection and spirituality. My faith deepens and becomes stronger when I am in Asia. God seems very near at hand when I am alone in the remote corners of this part of the world.

The words flowed smoothly and quickly from my soul onto the pages of the journal. Occasionally they would soften, but still be legible, as a drop from the cold bottle or a drop of sweat from my forehead fell on the ink.

The noodles came, broad, dark with sauce, mixed with small pieces of chicken, a couple of small shrimp, some nondescript vegetables, and a slice of lime on top. The waitress, respecting my Western origin, placed a fork and spoon, wrapped in a pink paper napkin, beside me. She smiled when I ignored them and reached for a pair of chopsticks. A short-tailed cat, seeing the new plate on my table, drifted toward me, hoping for some tidbit. Swifts chittered restlessly from their night roost under the eaves of the shop. The street beside me was slowly coming to life as people drifted to the food stalls and restaurants, as much for social encounters as for meals. The musty taste of the noodles blended perfectly with that of the beer. I breathed deeply of the thick night air. It was good to be back.

Agus and the driver joined me at my table and ordered their supper. There is more mixing of Chinese and ethnic Malays in Indonesia than there is in Malaysia. In Malaysia, a Malay is almost never found in a Chinese restaurant. Both men ordered rice, chicken, small bowls of egg soup, and hot, sweet tea mixed with canned milk (*tea tarik*). We discussed plans for the next day's work on the river, finished our meals, and then returned to our hotel rooms.

My room was very hot. I opened the window to its full extent and then, undressing, ducked under the mosquito net hanging over my bed and lay sweating on top of the sheets. There was temptation to turn on the tiny portable fan in the room, but it would drown out the night noises that are so precious to me when I'm in the tropics. Lying there in bed, in the quiet of my room, I could hear the tonking of nightjars coming from the little clump of forest beside the hotel and the ever so faint sound of music from the town's main street. I loved that blend. My thoughts drifted to the river and to the unknown elements for the coming day . . . and to my family on the opposite side of the world. It is always this way for me . . . imagining what can happen on a large river yet knowing that once on the water, my focus will be so intent that the chance for mishap is very slight. I live and work in a world of swirling water and boats. The big, brown rivers speak messages to me. I respect them as much or more than I love them. But still the thoughts swirl and it takes time to settle into sleep.

The predawn call to prayer stirred me. I stretched, rolled out of the bed, turned on the light in my room, and dressed. I knew that my companions would be up now and at prayer. Soon thereafter we'd meet for a quick breakfast and then be on our way, down to the river and to the boat. It would only be a day trip, perhaps twenty or thirty miles up the river and back, but still I packed my satchel for the unknown, just in case things didn't go as planned. I could hear the occasional whine of small motorcycles as the day came to life. It was still an hour until sunrise.

Breakfast consisted of fried bread mixed with egg (*roti telor*), with curry sauce on the side, and a tall *glass* (no cups here, please) of hot, sticky, sweet, milk tea. It is a breakfast that I've come to respect. In fact, I've sort of become addicted to it. It opens the eyes and sticks to the ribs. It alone is sufficient reason for me to keep returning to Southeast Asia. It is wonderful stuff and outstanding "gut wadding." A man can go all day on a breakfast like that . . . and I frequently have.

After breakfast we made our way down to the boat. Preparations were already underway. The boat was just a small seventeen-foot fiberglass "ski" boat with a single 45 horsepower outboard engine. It had a canopy that could be raised in the case of rain or to avoid the midday sun. Several small plastic containers of fuel were loaded into the forward compartment along with a box containing bottled water. Food for the day was placed into a plastic chest along with a block of ice. There were no life jackets and only a single paddle. I knew it was useless to ask for life jackets. There probably were none in the entire town. But I demanded that we find at least two more paddles. The men around me laughed and said the extra paddles were not needed because we'd be just fine in this dependable boat (*Inshallah*, "God willing"). I stood firm with my request, and the extra paddles were loaded.

The driver started the outboard and it purred beautifully. The men on the pier all smiled. I grinned back and, pointing to the paddles, said to the men, "Munkin saya akan digunakan ini untuk bersilat dengan buya" (Perhaps I can use them to fight off crocodiles). They all laughed and then we were cast off.

The current swept us out into the channel and for a moment we drifted downstream. Then the driver moved the throttle forward and we began moving upstream. There were small frame houses all along the river's banks. Below them boats were tethered. Most had nets in them, evidence that their owners were engaged in exploiting the river's fisheries resources and, subsequently, confirmation that my purposes for being on the river were justified. Women were washing clothes and dishes in the rivers and small children played in the shallows. Pollution was not an issue because the next *kampongs* (villages) were many miles upstream and they tended to be small and scattered.

From time to time I could see monkeys and hornbills moving among the trees. There were occasional splashes as crocodiles slipped into the water. River boats passed us going both ways. Some were floating homes and some were obviously taxis or engaged in the businesses of fishing or logging. In this last regard, it was obvious that timber was being extracted from the jungle in huge quantities. Large rafts of logs bound together by steel cable drifted downstream, guided (somewhat) by fairly insubstantial motorboats. I frequently saw the rafts piled up along the shores, disarticulated and from all appearances very much abandoned. The waste seemed incredible, but then, this was frontier, and such places encourage a mindset of inexhaustible resources. It was simply easier to go back and cut more than to try to take apart and put back into order the jumble of logs from wrecked rafts.

The sun played on the smooth surface of the water. There was as yet no wind. The breezes would come later in the morning and then die during the midday heat. Typically, they would only be resurrected by the brief but intense storms that are so common on tropical afternoons. The humming of the outboard and the reflections of jungle on the water ushered me into a trance-like state of semi-consciousness. I was awake but very much in the dreamtime. My thoughts drifted across the sandbars and into the shadowy places. The only time I was stirred from this state was when our driver would make a sudden sharp correction in order to avoid a log or other obstruction adrift in the currents.

We droned on for hours. The sun baked us and the wind dried us. By midday we'd made a serious dent in our supply of bottled water. Then, rounding a bend, we spotted a collection of floating houses. We motored up to them and I discovered that it was in fact a frontier way station, complete with store and a restaurant of sorts. We secured our boat to one of the mooring posts and climbed out, stretching and stomping to get back our land legs.

When I entered the station, it was so dark inside that for a few moments I couldn't see a thing. So I just stood inside the entryway until my eyes adjusted from hours of being out in the tropical sunlight. Once I could see, I had to grin to myself. These places are pretty much all alike. It doesn't matter if they are in Africa, Asia, or Alaska, these frontier outposts always have some grizzled man rumbling around behind a counter, a couple of vagabonds gathered at a table drinking something, and a young woman doing her best to keep things presentable. Sacks of staples sat on elevated platforms (to keep the moisture from spoiling the contents). Spools of rope were tucked into corners. Tools hung on the walls next to expired calendars. Big working knives, boxes of shotgun shells, and fishing gear completed the inventory.

You can order a simple meal and something to drink in most of these places, but it will take awhile to get served. Time has little bearing on activities. We ordered soup and tea (always hot). There was sugar for the tea, but no milk, not even the canned stuff. We sat at the table with the two men who had been there when we arrived. There were a few gelatinous pastries on a plate, covered by a big plastic, serrated cover to keep the flies off them. Indonesian pastries typically are very good, and these were no exception. They are sort of a half cake, half custard, with the consistency of a heavy, moist brownie or piece of fudge. Sometimes they have a dusting of shredded coconut, but more often they're just plain. They come in many colors, but most commonly they are green or yellowish brown.

The soup arrived hot and spicy. It was mostly broth, but down in the bottom was a little piece of chicken, a sort of dumpling, and a few sprigs of green vegetable. The first spoonful cleared my sinuses and swept away any vestiges of drowsiness lingering from my sun-induced trance. It's good stuff. In fact, it is very hard to find food in Southeast Asia that is not good. And, in spite of the seeming unconcern regarding cleanliness and good order that is typical of places like this river outpost, good hygiene in the preparation of food can always be counted on.

Being a Westerner, I aroused curiosity among the folks in the station. They talked past me, directing their conversation and their questions to my Indonesian companions. When I spoke to them in Bahasa, they were shocked. For a "European" to be here at all was a rare event, but to have one who spoke their language was beyond belief. Eventually, however, good conversation followed, and everybody was talking about fish and fisheries in the river. They naturally thought I was there to collect the valuable Arawana fish for the aquarium trade. Arawana were certainly available for the taking, but the more valuable red ones were increasingly hard to find. A large red Arawana could be sold in Jakarta or Singapore for many thousands of rupiah.

I explained that I was not here to collect their fish but rather to take a hard look at the fisheries that supplied fish products to regional fish markets. They nodded in approval and said that I'd come at the right time . . . the river was now in its banks and the fish that had been out in the floods were packed in the channels.

"Dimana ada orang-orang nalayian?" (Where are the fishermen?), I asked, for I'd hardly seen any on my trip upstream so far.

"Atas, jauh" (Higher and further), they answered.

This I'd expected because upstream was where the river's principal floodplain was located. This is where the fish would first be concentrated before making any downstream movements.

Finishing our lunch, we said good-bye all around, shook hands the typical Muslim way (each person gently taking both hands of the other then releasing them and touching the heart), and ambled out to our boat. We had many miles yet to go.

It was then that I began to have questions that I kept to myself: "How much further? How much time?"

Off we went, in search of the fishermen. We passed a few. Most were concentrated in small bays where tributary streams entered the main channel of the Kapuas. We spoke briefly with each group, surveyed their catch, recorded our data, and then moved on. These small groups were not the main body of fishermen. We pushed further upstream. The afternoon softened. There were only a few puffy clouds in the sky. Occasionally we'd pass a small, isolated house and, due to the hour, would notice that evening cooking fires were going and chores were underway. I resigned myself to the reality that we would not be going home that night. But little did I know . . .

Finally, as the sun was low on the horizon, we rounded a bend and encountered the main assemblage of fishermen. It was an incredible sight.

There were literally hundreds of boats, and in each boat there would be two or three fishermen. Most of the boats were brightly painted. A few had carved ornate figures on their bows. But it was the fishing gear that most impressed me. Each boat had a huge dip net. The mouth of the nets would be six to eight feet wide and perhaps ten to twelve feet long. The entire thing was attached to a long handle.

One man would move the boat around while the other would dip and harvest. And the catches were incredible. There was a decent diversity of fish species, but most of the catch was "Belida" (featherbacks). These were beautiful fish. Most were two to three feet long, silvery, with tapered bodies and strongly muscled sides and backs. Their heads were sort of "sloped down," much like a crappie back in North America, and, in fact, featherbacks tend to fill the same ecological niche.

It was then that I realized the *real* mission of the boat operator and his helper. Agus and I had come to conduct fisheries work. But the operator and his helper were here to buy valuable fish to be sold at very high price back in the town downstream. As I watched, they began to bargain with the fishermen and then to load the boat with fish.

I really didn't mind, but I wondered how they were going to keep the fish fresh overnight and during our trip downstream tomorrow. Obviously, we would be spending the night here or nearby in a fisherman's camp.

But I was informed that we would be going back downstream to the town *tonight*. And then the sun set.

I was concerned and told them so. My concerns fell on deaf ears. I switched into command mode and gave clear instructions that we would *not* be traveling on the river at night. My words still fell on deaf ears. Then I said that if they decided to travel at night, they would not be paid. This got their attention, but only to inform me that the pay that they would lose from me was insignificant compared to what they would earn by selling those fish.

And so there I was, with mutiny on my hands. They said that Agus and I could get out of the boat if we wanted and stay with the fishermen in their camps, or we could go home tonight with the operator and his helper. They didn't care one way or the other. But *they* were going home tonight.

Agus and I had a private council and decided that as dangerous as it was, it was far better and probably safer for us to stay with our boat and go back to the town that night. At most it would be a six- to eight-hour trip. The Kapuas was a big river and a full moon was scheduled to rise later in the evening. These guys seemed to know the river well and obviously would be prepared for night travel because they'd been planning this all along. So we said, "OK," and settled down for the trip. The operator and his helper just shrugged, finished loading their fish, and started the motor.

Darkness fell swiftly and the moon came up. It was fairly bright out in the main channel, but still I thought it wise for the operator to get out his light so that I could help him spot snags, logs, and other dangerous items. He said that he didn't have a light, that the moon was enough for him. I was astounded and pushed the issue. Finally, he pulled out a broad-beamed lantern, but the batteries were so weak that about all it could do was give us a general idea of where the riverbanks might be.

This was crazy! Driving down this huge tropical river in the night with no light and heavily loaded with fish was insane. But there was no place to go. In the middle of the Borneo jungle you don't just get out of the vehicle and flag down a taxi. Agus and I were conscripted for the duration. All we could do was hunker down in our corner of the boat, pray, and hope for the best. At least we had the blessing of the moon.

After an hour or so, I dozed off to sleep. I don't know how long I slept, but I was awakened by a shifting sound against the hull of our boat. There was no longer the smooth swish of hull on slick water. Rather, there was a hard-beating chop. I looked up at the sky. There was no moon and no stars. There was a steady wind that had kicked up the river's surface into small waves. The wind was getting stronger and occasionally had gusts. Then there was a clap of thunder and the rain began. The operator pulled up the boat's canopy and kept on driving. The only thing to do was to pull over to the riverbank and tie up until the storm passed. But I couldn't see the bank. Neither could the operator or anybody else in the boat. I shouted for him to cut off the engine and just let the boat drift—drifting was much safer than moving under power. But he wouldn't listen to me. He kept surging ahead, hell bent on getting his precious cargo to town in time to make tomorrow's morning market.

Then we ran over a log and nearly capsized. We carefully checked the boat. Thankfully, there were no holes. Surely that would teach the man a lesson, but it didn't. He cranked up the boat again, but this time only traveled at half throttle. Then we ran headlong into the riverbank. He backed out, modified course, and rammed into the bank on the other side.

That did it. I jumped to my feet, grabbed him by the shoulders, gave him a hard shake, and told him in no uncertain terms to stop the boat—NOW! He struggled momentarily and I overpowered him. I held him down and told him that if he didn't want me to throw him out of the boat and leave him out there in the dark river, he would accept my command, and that if he attempted to fight me, I might be forced to do the unthinkable . . . be forced to kill him.

I was deadly serious and he quickly realized that I'd meant every word I'd spoken. His helper was cowering, curled up in a corner of the boat, shaking, scared out of his mind. I don't know if he was scared of the raging storm that enveloped us or scared of the storm that had just erupted from me.

"Boleh Tuan, Boleh" (OK, Lord, OK).

"Now," I said, "Start the motor, move to open water, and put that throttle at idle speed. If I say stop, you stop. Do you understand?"

"Boleh Tuan, Boleh."

The storm on the river reached a tempest. Waves crashed over the boat. I instructed the operator to move the boat to the edge of the river and to tie up. He did as told. But it was a place where the channel was straight and, subsequently, there was no sand bar with slack water. It didn't matter. We had to stop.

We found a root sticking out of the high mud bank and tied to it, with the storm crashing all around and water surging beneath. If we were struck by a floating log, the boat, with our heavy load of fish, would probably capsize and sink, and we would be thrown into the water. There was little question about that. So in desperation I scoured the boat for anything that would float, anything that I could hold onto in the event of a capsized boat. The light with weak batteries had long since faded. All I could do was grope around, searching by feel. I found an empty plastic container, then another, then another. Then I found pieces of rope. I called Agus to my side and instructed him on how to convert those containers to life preservers and how to tie them onto our bodies. Both of us had three containers: two across our chests and one on our back. That way, if we were knocked unconscious, our faces would be above the water and we would probably not drown. I didn't bother to see if the operator and his buddy were doing anything similar . . . and I didn't care.

The storm lasted for another hour or so. The boat filled with water and we had to find other containers to bail with. It was then that I asked the operator about the containers. I didn't remember seeing empty containers in the boat when we'd loaded that morning. He wouldn't answer me. Then I realized what had happened.

He obviously hadn't had money to pay for the fish he'd gotten during his bargaining sessions. He'd bought the fish with our fuel and had slyly been able to make the transactions without me noticing, with the fishermen off-loading the fuel into other containers and passing the empties back. I'd been paying so much attention to the waning hour and to the fish in the boat that I hadn't even noticed.

"Ada ka cucup mynak untuk balik" (Do we have enough fuel to get back)?

"Tak tahu Tuan" (I don't know, Lord).

After the storm passed and we bailed the boat one more time, the operator started the motor and we were on our way again . . . slowly, even with the help of the moon that had again decided to bless us with a little light. We traveled about another hour. Then the motor started to race and sputter. We were running out of gas.

A few moments later, we were enveloped by the stillness of a tropical night, adrift on the river. I grabbed two paddles, handed one to the operator and one to his helper.

"Ke duaduana, naik dihadapan dan mula berkerja" (Both of you, get up front and start working), I said.

"Apaka tentang yang ketiga?" (What about the third one?), he asked, pointing to the last paddle in my hand.

"Itu illiah untuk membuno awak kalau awak berhenti berkerja" (It is to kill you with if you stop working).

They started paddling.

I let them take a ten-minute break every hour. After three hours we spotted a light. It was the light of the frontier station where we'd had lunch. The operator said we should go there. I said OK, but to be quiet and not wake them up . . . that we would tie up and wait until dawn and then, hopefully, get some fuel. I figured that the proprietor would be armed and in the wee hours of the morning wouldn't ask many questions before shooting.

We quietly eased up to the dock as I'd instructed. But as soon as we were tied up, the operator jumped from the boat, ran to the proprietor's hut, and started pounding on the door. "Bangun, bangun" (Get up, get up), he shouted. I was furious but said nothing.

An oil lantern came on, and slowly, cautiously, the proprietor approached the door, single-barreled shotgun in hand. But then, bless his heart, recognizing us, he came on out and sold us enough fuel to get home. I paid him double what he asked.

There was a faint grayness to the sky by the time we were back on the river. Slowly, from the center of the river channel, we began to see the dark outline of forest on either side of the river and the V-shaped ripples of snags that lay just under the water's surface. The more we could see, the faster the operator drove the boat. I just let him do as he wished.

Three hours later we pulled up to the dock in the town. I said nothing at all. I just jumped out of the boat, walked directly to the Chinese restaurant, and bought a large beer.

While sitting there I saw Agus walking up the street and asked him if he was OK. He said he was fine, still shaking a little, very tired, cold, wet, but otherwise fine. I finished my beer and went to my room. Throwing my soaked gear and clothing into a corner of the room, I wrapped myself in my sarong, walked down to the end of the hall, and took a mandi. I'd just returned to my room after the shower when there was a knock at my door.

I opened it, and there stood the boat operator with a cocky, one-sided grin on his face. Then he spoke: "Saya mahu duit saya . . . TUAN . . . malam tadi sudah banyak kras" (I want my pay . . . LORD . . . last night was pretty rough).

I stood there for a few moments, looking at him and his cocky grin, and was completely dumbfounded. Coolly and deliberately I walked through my door out into the hall, and without holding back, I slammed him into the wall. Then I backed off. He staggered momentarily and slid down onto the floor. Then, after shaking his head, he got up without a word, made his way down the hall, and stumbled down the stairs. I shut the door to my room and went to bed.

Later that day, after a few hours of very deep and welcomed sleep, I ambled out of the hotel and down to the riverfront. There was a little *kedai* (shop) perched over the docking area that served cold lemonade. I bought a glass and sat down to watch the boats and the fishmongers. I recognized our boat at the end of the line of boats and saw that a crowd had gathered around it. Then I saw Agus emerge from the crowd. He walked up the pier toward the kedai and spotted me.

"How goes the fish selling, Agus?"

"Very good my friend. He is getting high prices . . . and he's telling everyone about his great courage, fighting to save the Tuan from robbers during the storm last night, and how he had to battle the river as well as the robbers in order to bring the Tuan and the fish back to the town. He has a big lump on the back of his head from the fighting and is a bit of a hero right now. I wonder how he got that lump?"

Setting down my glass of lemonade, I stroked my beard and said, "Agus, I just wouldn't know . . . I just wouldn't know."

Agus broke into a grin and spoke to me again, this time in Bahasa, "Ada susuai . . . adala susuai. Allah akbar kawan saya" (As things should be . . . as things really should be. God is great, my friend).

"You are correct my friend. God is truly great. We made it back alive. I can assure you, however, that the lump is from the mortal realm."

Agus grinned again. "Allah Akbar."

The Hardest Hunt

The western shore of Cook Inlet slipped out of sight below me. Ahead lay the mountain passes and then beyond them the sprawling country west of Lake Clark where Dean Rhine and I would hunt caribou. Years before, I'd served on the faculty of the University of Alaska and that was where I'd met Dean. Back then we'd hunted ptarmigan together in the hills east of Fairbanks, and a couple of years back we'd hunted black bear together in the forests surrounding Prince William Sound. We'd used Dean's boat for that hunt. This caribou hunt was, however, our first fly-in hunt together. It was a late season hunt and we'd been warned that if the weather soured we might have to tough it out for a while until a rescue could be organized. Floatplanes do not land on ice, and so the risk was very real.

The pilot motioned to us as we entered the mountain passes, sweeping his arms in a broad gesture. Glaciers hung in nearly every valley and there were Dall sheep scattered on the steep slopes. The roar of the Beaver's engine prevented us from doing much talking, so we just pointed at what we saw around us in the landscape and grinned at each other. Our destiny was Whitefish Lake, a hundred miles or so north of Lake Iliamna. We'd be dropped off there, and if luck and weather held, we'd be picked up a week later.

As we flew through the mountains the weather began showing signs of closing in. The pilot became quieter and it seemed that he was becoming more and more anxious. Typically on fly-in hunts like this a pilot will give you a "fly around" so that you can get a feel for the land you'll be hunting. But this time the pilot took us directly to the lake, made the landing, pulled up as close as he could to the shore, and without a word started helping us get our gear out of the plane. Dean and I were wearing hip boots. The pilot would hand us a piece of gear or a pack or a rifle case and we'd slosh ashore with it, making a pile. Once the plane was unloaded, the pilot confirmed our pickup date, said a quick good-bye, and left us.

We were not in caribou country. We were in a mucky, black spruce bog, laced with tiny creeks, muskeg and dead snags. It was terrain for moose and ducks and maybe black bear, but not caribou. But to the north however were hills, and we realized that it was there that we'd have to go if we were to have any chance at all of a successful caribou hunt. Now, the business at hand was to get our camp set up before the weather that had so worried the pilot closed in on us.

I'd brought my mountain tent and Dean had a tarp. The mountain tent was shelter, but the tarp would provide us elbow room. The spongy ground would not hold stakes to anchor the tent, but we'd expected this and had plenty of rope, particularly for the tarp. The tent, since it had an external frame, would pretty much stay put without stakes as long as we kept gear inside it. After setting up the tent and tarp, we took our food beyond camp and hoisted it in waterproof bear bags up into the top branches of a spruce.

Within a couple of hours we'd converted a patch of Alaska into our home. As I looked around the camp and the awesome scenery that surrounded us, I took a deep breath and felt myself reconnect with this great land.

Dean brought out food from our cache and I fired up our little gas stove. Soon we had water boiling for tea and food ready for cooking. The chilled, damp air cleared the lingering dust from the haunts of men from my body and my mind. The lead-colored sky with swirling fog filling the mountain passes, coupled with a quiet that was so thick I could almost feel it, enveloped me in the wildness, the rawness, the awesome remoteness into which I'd plunged. And as always when I'm in such places, particularly when they're in Alaska, I felt energy swell inside of me, and my mind seemed to clear itself of all sorts of internal dialogue.

I stood there, hot cup of tea in my hands, just looking, feeling, praying a little, and hoping for a good hunt . . . a safe hunt. If an accident occurred, there was no way to make contact with the outside. We had no radio and this was before the day of satellite telephones. A simple infection from a cut or a broken bone could be deadly. We had to be careful even as we pushed ourselves on the hunt.

Mid-September in Alaska has pretty short days. And each day loses several minutes on both ends compared to the one before it. As dusk settled on us I made a quick reconnaissance trip around our camp area and out toward the hills where we'd be hunting. We were in a pretty mucky area, and the situation didn't seem to change much for a long way as I moved in the direction of the hills. There were lots of creeks meandering here and there, but most were small and easily crossed, either by jumping or by fallen trees. But it would take time to get to good hunting areas . . . probably two to three hours at the least. And then we'd have to quit hunting in time to make the two- to three-hour hike back to camp. At best we'd have four or five hours of hunting time each day. That wasn't very much, but it would have to do.

Returning to our camp, I found Dean already in his sleeping bag, reading a novel by the beam from his flashlight. Beside him lay his .44 magnum revolver. My .357 revolver was on my belt. This was grizzly as well as black bear country, and bears, regardless of type, are taken very seriously. Our rifles also were handy, with rounds in the magazines but nothing chambered. When situations develop, seconds count. I checked my rifle and laid it beside my sleeping bag. It's an old Winchester .30-06 that has been a faithful companion on many hunts. But nevertheless, I always think about how small the hole in the end of my rifle's barrel is when I'm on an Alaskan hunt. It's got plenty of punch, but still . . .

The wind freshened and caused the tarp to flap and the tent to strain. A few misty drops of cold rain splattered against the rain fly. There was a dampness that penetrated everything. I undressed, placed my boots just inside the tent by its door and slid down into the icy, clammy bag. But within a few minutes the bag had warmed and I too was reading by flashlight. On trips like this, particularly when there is every likelihood that you can become stranded for long periods of time, big, thick novels are the order of the day. Typically, you bring books that you simply cannot bring yourself to read anyplace else. I brought two by John Steinbeck: *The Grapes of Wrath* and *Cannery Row*. Once I got into them, they were not as challenging as I'd anticipated.

The next morning after a quick breakfast, we donned day packs, grabbed our rifles, and began the journey up to the hills. Beyond the first series of creeks, the land opened up a little, giving us visual "breathing room," which is a comfort in grizzly country. We also made a point of talking a lot so that if there were bears around they'd know we were coming. Surprise encounters are not healthy.

Solid, reliable, dependable gear is essential on an Alaskan hunt. Rifle, waterproof boots, rain gear, shelter, and a sleeping bag are absolutes. Since we were just making day hunts, returning each day to our camp, we didn't bother weighting ourselves down with a shelter and sleeping bag. We'd need the space in our packs to haul our caribou back to camp. While that would make perfect sense perhaps anyplace else in the world, we both knew that there was a real risk here in Alaska. But it was a risk we decided to take.

Once we arrived at the base of the hills, walking got a lot easier. Here the ground was solid. There were no muskeg tussocks, no hidden trenches full of water, no springy footing. We moved higher and higher, through boulder fields, along canyons, skirting the faces of cliffs and forcing our way through alder thickets. Finally we arrived in the high country and the entire world opened up to us. Although we could not see our camp, we could see the place along Whitefish Lake where it was located. In the distance we could see the mountains and the shadowy outline of Lake Iliamna. All around us lay mountain tundra. Frost had already brushed these hills and they were flush with color. The reds and oranges and yellows seemed to dance before our eyes. The sky cleared and the sun warmed us to the point that we doffed our coats and hunted only in our shirtsleeves. A gentle breeze brushed us off and on. We encountered an old porcupine, and nothing would do but for Dean to harass it a little until it stopped and bared its quills. Then we moved on and settled in a jumble of rocks for lunch.

This place was supposed to be thick with caribou. There was sign everywhere, but no animals. We pulled out our binoculars and glassed all of the country around us, but still the land looked lifeless except for a few ptarmigan and the occasional falcon. Then, far away on a distant horizon, we saw a lone caribou bull. At least we saw the rear end of a lone caribou bull. He was in the process of leaving our lives forever.

Mid-afternoon came and we knew that we had to start back down the mountain. Following the lay of the land, we were able to navigate easily and in less than two hours were back in camp. Everything there was still in order. We'd had no bears. For this we were thankful. We quickly prepared supper, checked our food cache, and crawled into our sleeping bags. But this evening there was no reading. It had been a long day.

The next two days we repeated this schedule. One of the days was plagued by wind and rain, but the other was a fine, clear, cold Alaskan autumn day. But we saw no caribou. Apparently, they'd already migrated through this area. Our hunt was starting to develop into a first-class bust as far as game harvest was concerned. And the long hikes up into the hills and the return to camp, racing the fading day, were taking their toll on us. Something had to change. So we decided to pack in equipment for a spike camp up in the hills and hunt from the spike camp rather than make the round-trip journey each day from and back to our base camp. We figured that we'd need supplies for at least three days. Also, we both expressed some relief that in the event of problems, we'd have a camp much closer to where we'd be hunting.

After setting up our spike camp the following morning, we still had several hours of hunting time left, particularly since we would not have to leave the hills by mid-afternoon. We also moved higher than on previous days and finally found a spot for lunch that gave us a good vantage point. We leaned against rocks with sandwiches, granola, canteens, and chocolate bars at hand and munched as we glassed the tundra around us. Suddenly Dean whispered, "Don, there are two bulls just 300 yards from us, bedded down. Take a look!"

I slithered over to him and looked to the spot where he was pointing. Sure enough, there were two bull caribou. One had fairly small antlers, but the other was a dandy, with tall thick beams and double shovels.

The clock was ticking on our hunt. The pilot was scheduled to pick us up in three days. These were the only caribou we'd seen except for that lone bull our first day out. We figured that this was probably our only chance to take caribou on this hunt.

Since Dean had spotted the bulls, he would take the bigger of the two and I would take the smaller one. Other than antler size, however, they were pretty much the same. Both of them would weigh around 350 pounds.

We left our day packs among the rocks, grabbed our rifles, and stuffed a few extra rounds into our hip pockets. Slowly we slipped down and around the rocks and into a small ravine that we figured would take us to within 100 yards of the bulls. The wind was in our favor and the bulls were facing away from us. The setup was perfect.

When we topped the edge of the ravine we had some large rocks ahead of us that served as perfect cover for our final approach. As quietly as we could we eased into position and looked around the sides of the big rock that would be our ambush site. The bulls were still there, but now standing and around 120 yards away. That was fine. Our rifles were sighted in for 200 yards and we were both comfortable shooting at that range. We needed to be quick, however, because it was apparent that the bulls were getting ready to move out of the area.

We quietly jacked rounds into the chambers of our rifles and agreed that on the count of three (Dean counting) we'd fire. Using our sweaters for rests, we laid our rifles on top of the large rock, lined up the cross hairs of our scopes on our bulls, and at the count of three fired.

From the corner of my eye I saw Dean's bull crumple. But my bull took off snorting and blowing steam. I jacked another round into my rifle, aimed, fired, and somehow missed again. The caribou picked up the pace and was gathering speed. The thought passed through my mind that I was just about to screw up what might be my one and only chance to shoot a caribou. I heard Dean mention something about him shooting the bull for me, but I didn't respond. By this time the bull was at least 300 yards away and quartering away from me. The image of that magnificent animal, head back, snorting steam, almost prancing across the tundra out there on that hillside, is one that is permanently etched in my mind.

Breathing deeply, I settled down and let all of my training and experience in rifle shooting take over. Holding steady, I took a deep breath and let it out. The bull continued to pick up speed and distance. I took another deep breath, let half of it out, held the cross hairs of the scope a foot in front of the bull and four inches high, and squeezed the trigger.

The bullet hit the bull at the base of his neck and he almost flipped over himself, dead on the spot. The distance was almost 350 yards. I could see him lying on his side out there, gray and white and very still against the red and orange tundra as the day began to fade around us. Dean slapped me on the back and congratulated me on the shot. To this day I do not know how I missed a bull caribou twice at 120 yards. But my final shot, the one that brought him down, the one where I "kicked in" as a rifle shooter, was the only hit on the bull.

A chill settled on the hills as twilight approached. But Alaskan twilights are prolonged, so we had time to process our animals. Within an hour we had both bulls field dressed, skinned, and mostly boned out. We were joined by a red fox that would creep up to me as I worked, trying to steal scraps. I occasionally tossed him a chunk of meat and then tossed him a bone with a few strips of meat still clinging to it. This was the prize that the fox had been waiting for, and once he had it he took off for his home.

Wrapping the meat back inside of the caribou hides and placing the meat and heads off to the side a hundred yards or so away from the gut piles, we left it all, planning to return the following morning to begin the job of packing everything down off of the hill. The temperature was below freezing, so the meat would not spoil. The only concern was that of bears or perhaps wolverines finding the kills during the night. Hopefully, if this happened, they'd stay on the gut piles and leave the meat alone. It is just one of the realities of hunting in Alaska. And . . . if there is a bear on your kill when you return to it, the kill, by law, belongs to the bear. The bear cannot be shot unless you happen to have a bear tag. Dean had a tag, but neither of us wanted to kill a bear on this hunt. We'd just accept reality and give our kill to the bear if it happened.

It was starting to get dark and there was a west wind picking up as we worked our way back across the hills, through a ravine choked with alders, and back on the slope where we'd made our spike camp. Clouds moved in and the wind got stronger. It finally got so dark that we could not see where we were going and had to stop. There were cliffs and loose rock on this hillside. We had to stop or risk a serious accident. There was no choice.

So here we were, on an Alaskan hillside with cold wind blasting us, smelling of freshly killed caribou, without shelter, without sleeping bags, and with only a couple of granola bars and two canteens of water. We found a place beside a big rock surrounded by some thick spruce trees that blocked the wind a little. We ate the granola, drank some water, and then sat back-to-back, trying to conserve heat. We had one of those thin portable "space blankets" and wrapped it around us to help block more of the wind and to capture a little more of our body heat. A fire was out of the question with the wind. We didn't want to create a situation where we'd be chased off the mountain by a forest or brush fire. So we just sat there; we told stories, sang songs, tried anything we could to stay awake, with rifles loaded, ready for bear. It was a very long, very miserable night and resulted in me developing a list of things that absolutely must be in a survival pack (including an emergency "space blanket" sleeping bag) and be taken with you regardless of where you go (and when I got back home to Mississippi I made just such a pack and have it with me . . . *always*).

When dawn finally crept on the hills, the day was clear and frosty and still. We found that we were within 200 yards of our spike camp. We'd deal with the meat later. We plunged into our sleeping bags inside the little tent and slept for hours. It was midday when we woke up, cooked a meal, and grabbed packs and rifles to go get the meat.

Everything was intact when we got to the meat. Blessings come in all forms. The first order of business was hauling meat and antlers to the spike camp. It took all the rest of the day to do that. The following day we packed meat and gear back to the base camp. It took four trips to complete this task. We were exhausted but full of satisfaction for having pulled off the feat in just one day.

With the meat and antlers secured and hanging out of reach of bears in tall trees, we settled into camp life, anxious for our pickup the following day. But it never happened. It fact, it didn't happen for nearly a week. By that time we'd finished all of our food that we'd brought with us, except tea and a little oil, and were shooting grouse for the pot with bird shot loads from our revolvers. We also started eating some of our caribou.

The whole area was covered with thick fog. We couldn't see the hills to the north. We couldn't see across the lake. In fact, from our camp, we couldn't even see the lake. We were socked in.

It was impossible weather to fly in and we knew it. We also knew that the weather in the mountain passes was probably worse than where we were and that the pilot's earlier warning might prove to be reality. Ice was beginning to form around the edges of Whitefish Lake. If we got a cold snap, the lake would quickly freeze, and then we'd have to be rescued by helicopter. We knew that time was of the essence. As long as we had fog, there was little likelihood of a freeze up. But once it cleared, the situation could change fast.

We lay in our tent, listening to water dripping from the spruce trees onto the tarp and rain fly, reading our books, occasionally wiping down our rifles with oily rags to help keep them from rusting, every now and then getting up and hunting grouse, and once getting up with rifles to defend ourselves from a prowling bear that turned out to be a love-sick moose.

The days were long . . . but the nights were longer. The inside of our tent, our little world, became sort of a nest, secure, relatively warm, and certainly dry and out of the wind. The hours drifted along with hardly a word spoken. Occasionally, a journal would open and there would be some scratching with a pen. It's all part of the reality of being out doing stuff in the Alaska bush that isn't talked about much: the time in tents . . . the preciousness of shelter . . . the prospects of encounters with beasts (some of which bite), with persons who are coming to get you, and sometimes with those who just wander by (always a shock, at least to me), people just out and about, wayward sojourners, trappers, other hunters. They are rare, but they're out there. It did not happen on this hunt, but it happened to me once while hunting up above the Brooks Range in the Arctic National Wildlife Refuge and another time over in the Yukon. And when these folks show up, you have to make room in your tent for them. It's the unwritten, unspoken law of the North. And you feed them too. It is just like you never leave your cabin locked and you never leave it without a good supply of dry wood and some food (if you have any) just in case someone comes through who needs shelter and warmth and something to eat. And when they leave, they are supposed to be sure that the cabin is ready for the next person who might come by.

We ran out of oil and began boiling chunks of grouse and caribou meat. We reused tea until we could get no color from it. The batteries for our flashlights finally failed. We started counting matches and studying maps. Beyond the hills to the northwest about forty miles lay a tiny settlement called Lime Village, and to the west-northwest about the same distance away was a small Air Force station. They'd be long walks but possible, if necessary. We knew the way and were certainly equipped and able to handle such a trip.

Occasionally, we thought we heard plane engines, but the sound always seemed to fade the harder we listened. Finally, after waiting nearly a week in camp, the sound was for real. The sky was clearing and the plane was coming. We saw it circle once, then down it came, pontoons skimming on the surface of the lake. Most of our stuff, including our meat, was already packed and ready for loading down by the lake by the time the plane made it to the shoreline near our camp. All we needed to do was take down the tent and pack up sleeping bags. When we met the pilot, he was in hip boots, tying up his plane at the edge of the lake. He told us that he'd tried several times to come get us out but had to turn back each time because there was bad weather in the mountain passes.

But, quite frankly, had it not been for the reality that we had basically run out of supplies, I would have just as soon stayed out there in the bush for a while longer. In my heart I really wasn't ready to leave and was sort of hoping that I'd have to hike out to Lime Village. I was growing stronger in body and spirit every day that I spent out there. Smoldering embers in my adventurer's soul were starting to blaze again. I just needed a few more days to complete the process.

Being stranded in a remote part of Alaska was for me something akin to Briar Rabbit being thrown into the Briar Patch. I liked it. I liked the feeling of being abandoned. I liked the fog, the howl of the wind, the damp cold, the hunt for game, the shooting, the packing of meat, the quiet, the stillness, the way the sun sparkles on frozen blueberries, the way a fox will trot up to you without fear, snatching pieces of the caribou you've just shot, the way the soil smells in a black spruce bog, the way brown, clear, tea-stained water in the creeks swirls in tiny pockets . . . I liked being in a world so huge, so wild, so awesomely, beautifully, lonely that it swallows the report of a rifle as if it were nothing more that the snapping of a twig.

I think this caribou hunt in the hills north of Whitefish Lake was my hardest big game hunt, and I've had many. But there is another hunt, a very desperate hunt that is much, much harder. It can consume us. It can destroy us. It can lead us to spectacular vistas and carry us to an awesome abyss. It is a hunt that can bring us our greatest joy and our greatest sadness. It is the hunt for self and place and spiritual connection to both. The clock ticks and we become more desperate as we slog through the muck, marshes, and tangles. Some give up. Some, like me, somehow, miraculously, succeed. We're able to break free from the places that suck at our boots and tear our clothing. We enter the high country where there is space and light and clear, crisp winds. We find the place that fits and the person that is truth . . . the way, the energy, and the vision that keep us moving on the hunter's sojourn. The reality is that a hunt never really ends. Rather, the hunter engages in an eternal, timeless process . . . forever seeking bigger game. As I roamed those hills above Whitefish Lake and traversed the trail between the hills and our base camp, with a freshly killed caribou lashed to my pack, rifle in hand, muscles working smoothly, and a song in my heart, I knew that the hunting of caribou had been but the framework for hunting this bigger game.

This hunt for bigger game first led me to Alaska nearly thirty years ago, back in the mid-1970s. As a young man full of spit and vinegar, dreams and energy, tossing security and safety to the winds as I roamed the earth, Alaska reached out and grabbed me with its powerful presence, its no-nonsense reality of life honed to a fine edge. I realized clearly and absolutely during that first venture to the far north that Alaska was the world where I belonged, a place where I fit.

Now, every time I go there I hear voices that tell me to stay. But I don't stay. I always leave. And then, eventually, I always return. I leave because there are so many other trails in a man's life, so many wines to taste, and so little time, and I leave because I am a restless vagabond. I am truly of the race of men that can't sit still, the men that Robert Service wrote about, the race of men that must roam the world at will. Yet I return, again and again, because Alaska has its powerful grip on me and will not turn me loose. And I know that it will ultimately win in the end. Alaska always does. I know this because when I'm back, when I'm out there in the Alaskan bush, I click into another mindset, another rhythm, and become a different man. He's the man (of the many who live in my oversoul) that I really like the best. Although he cranks into gear whenever I'm out on the currents of the world, regardless of setting or mission, he is most alive when he's in Alaska. And I know that he must be fed Alaska from time to time, or else he will wither into nothing more than a shadow and his voice will fade into a whisper.

So as long as I can scrounge a ticket, hoist a pack, and shoulder a gun, I will keep going back. As long as I can hear the winds of my soul and see visions of another way and smell the essence of earth and reach out and touch a freshly killed caribou, I will keep going back. As long as lonely land is there . . . I will keep going back. As long as the clock continues to tick for me, I will keep going back. I will . . . I will.

Southwest Conference

In my opinion Arkansas is just about as far west as a person can go in the United States before you start heading east again. By the time you're in California, you are all the way back East as far as I can tell. For that reason I never quite understood why the University of Arkansas was taken out of collegiate football's Southwest Conference (the only non-Texan university in the conference) and reassigned to the Southeast Conference. It just didn't make any sense to me. It wasn't so much the football that mattered to me. I'm a hunter and fisherman, a canoer and woods rambler, and not a big fan of competitive sports. It was more a matter of cultural values, identity, and common language. A football team is sort of like a flag. It tells folks who you are, what you stand for, and who you feel connected with, even if you don't fall into lockstep with the roaring crowds.

With Jackson as my last name and a family history that incorporates linkages to the old Confederacy, homesteading, and cotton farming, lots of people in the Deep South assume I'm in the "mint julep" and Spanish moss club. However, they are just not listening very closely to me when I talk. They think I'm speaking "Dixie." But listen again . . . there's a soft Southwestern "twang" in my speech . . . one that has persisted across the expanses of time, place, and cross-cultural forces. It is a blend of cowboy and Ozark mountain folk.

Similarly, men in the Southeastern United States think I share with them the same perspective with respect to what makes women beautiful. Wrong again. Surely there's something appealing when graceful Southern belles drift across the veranda exuding class and fine breeding . . . the product of generations of careful genetic selection (with wealthy men in charge of the process). But most women in the Deep South do not have the ability to wear blue jeans just right, nor do they have the sharper features, penetrating eyes, and high cheekbones that hint of just a shade of native blood adding spice to the mixture.

I also like to be in places where there's a bit of Spanish spoken, the fire and mystery of dark-eyed senoritas, a touch of below-the-border music, and the dedicated hardworking men and women from our southern neighbors who increasingly are responsible for keeping the United States going. Nowadays this is happening even in the part of Mississippi where I've lived for the past twenty-five years. But Arkansas and Texas had these treasures even before they became states.

The bottom line is that I can just go so long without reconnecting with my roots west of the Mississippi River. In fact, even when I've crossed the river, I still need to push on for a while and get into the hill country before the shift takes hold. But I can tell when I'm getting close to the world that strokes my heart. The trees begin to get short enough so that you could knock a fox squirrel from the top of most of them with a shotgun. This generally can't be done along the river or points east because most of the trees are too tall. And the fox squirrels I see along the road as I pull out of the Mississippi River floodplain and start coursing through the Ozarks and Ouachitas don't have the black faces that they typically have back East. Rather they're pretty much rusty orange blending with salt and pepper from tip to tail.

Once I edge into the Arkansas hills west of Little Rock, the creeks start to run clear because they have rock bottoms rather than mud bottoms. There are also proportionally more rifles than shotguns in the gun racks of pickup trucks. There's more of a dry, weathered look to rural houses, gas stations, and most people above the age of forty-five years. It seems also that there's less trash along the roads, but maybe it is just blown back from the road and into the bushes as a result of prairie winds or their derivatives. And most stock ponds I see in the west are smaller than the ones further east. It reflects a different balance, a different connection between landscape and climate.

During the spring of my fifty-fifth year the world really began to close in on me. Part was a factor of age and dealing with mortality in new ways. Part was political. Part was professional. Part was spiritual. I was getting boxed in on all sides and after a few months of battling my demons I started to feel myself slipping. There was a quiet crisis in my heart. The usual remedies didn't help: praying, walking in the woods, practicing pistol shooting, busting clay pigeons with my shotgun, burying myself in work. So, realizing that something had to be done to restore order and peace in my soul, I accepted an invitation to spend three days in Texas at Caddo Creek Ranch with a friend from Louisiana named Buddy Ball, his barber friend named Larry Bringle, and the owner of the ranch, Paul Calhoun. The ranch is located near a tiny crossroad called Poynor in East Texas about halfway between Tyler and Palestine and perhaps an hour or two east of Dallas. It's hill country, cattle country, and, here and there, timber country.

Paul had recently inherited the ranch from his grandfather, Vernon Calhoun. The ranch covered an expanse of rolling countryside totaling over four thousand acres. Within the ranch are located three lakes that are noted as being some of the best if not *the* best largemouth bass fishing in the entire nation. Fishing for bass on Caddo Creek Ranch is by invitation only. It is impossible to buy entry . . . regardless of professional, business, or political stature.

It was the medicine I desperately needed. I needed to reconnect with myself and a culture and with people and with land and water and sky and fishing in a big way, on big land. I needed big steaks, big burgers, big salads, big drinks, big tales, big smiles, big handshakes, and big heavens at night.

I knew that I was deep into the process of getting reconnected when I stopped at a Wal-Mart store in Atlanta, Texas, to pick up a few hooks, weights, plastic worms, and an ice chest. As I was standing in line there was a young woman with her little boy in front of me. I'd say that she was probably in her mid-twenties and the little boy was about three years old. She looked back at me and with a soft twang in her speech said that I needed to be in line in front of her since all I had was a little bit of stuff and she had a full basket. She had the sharp features of a Southwestern girl, and though small and obviously tired (young mothers are always tired), she projected the attractiveness and the energy of a person who lives close to the earth . . . a person connected in very real ways to the world around her. I accepted her offer, told her "thanks," and then spoke to her son. That seemed to make her happy. She smiled again and said it was her only young un' and that he was enough . . . no more young un's for her.

After I checked out and paid for my stuff, it was hard not to look back at her as I walked out of the store. I knew that to do so would have created a wrinkle in the encounter. But as I walked out across the parking lot to my truck, I took a deep breath and realized that there was a very deep goodness that literally oozed from that East Texas culture.

Onward I pressed, across thicket country, river bottoms, and hills. The land started to spread out. There was breathing room, more and more of it the further I traveled. Finally I came to the crossroads at Poynor, turned south for a mile or so, then west, following a sign that indicated the ranch lay about four miles ahead. The narrow, paved road to the ranch twisted among the hills and occasionally topped them, giving me a fine view of the land. When I arrived on the ranch I passed under a gateway that had the image of a cowboy kneeling in prayer, his horse beside him. I knew I was in the right place, physically and spiritually. I opened my heart and just let Texas flow into it. Then I drove to the boat ramp that was at the bottom of a hill on the largest of the ranch's three lakes. Buddy Ball had told me to meet him there so that we could start my sojourn with an evening of fishing.

After parking my truck, I walked down to an old, creaky, wooden pier. An elderly couple was on the pier fishing. I visited with them a little, not enough to break the spell, but enough to be sociable. They said that they had not caught anything, but I could tell it didn't really matter to them. They were trying to catch bluegill and crappie, but mostly I think they just liked being there on the lake, and being together. Looking out across the lake, I could see a boat with two fishermen in it. I dialed Buddy Ball's cell phone number and, sure enough, it was him and his friend Larry out there in the boat. They immediately started the boat and came to get me, with instructions over the cell phone for me to get all my fishing stuff down to the pier and get ready to catch bass. As they motored over I watched a scissor-tailed flycatcher flutter in the wind and an alligator cruise through some lily pads. The elderly couple quietly fished on the dock beside me. I could feel the demons within me losing their grip.

Buddy and Larry eased the boat up to the pier and I got in. Greetings were exchanged and I settled into a spot on the boat. We slowly motored to the western end of the four-hundred-acre lake and rigged up. Buddy and Larry were fishing spinner baits. But I looked over the water and decided that a weed-less plastic worm fished gently with the light touch of a spinning rod and rigged without a weight would be the ticket.

The wind ruffled the water. It brought rich earth smells to me. I looked up at the sky and watched a hawk soar. Purple gallinules, coots, and herons prowled the shallows. A fish swirled occasionally. Suddenly my line tightened and began to drift away. I lowered my rod, took up the slack, and slammed back to set the hook. A four-pound bass launched itself into the air and then tore across an open stretch of water. My spinning rod arched and the drag on the reel screeched. Texas bass have big pulls, big jumps, and big fight in them. The fish ripped around the lily pads, bore down into muck, and came up again, shaking its head. Finally I was able to work the fish to the side of the boat, where Larry netted the beast. My demons were frantic, knowing that they not only had lost their grip on me, but were being attacked and smashed. I just grinned.

The afternoon deepened into evening. The talk centered on fishing, boats, land, and friendships. I took deep breaths and kept casting into the water and into my soul. The strikes were coming fast and furious. With every bass I caught, another demon bit the dust. I looked around, at my friends, the lake, that wonderful land, and felt strength and focus returning. I realized that I'd been very close to an edge . . . that I'd almost waited too long to reconnect. "Never again," I told myself.

As the afternoon wind died I switched to a top-water plug. Those big Texas bass boiled and slashed and exploded all over that plug, and each time they did, another corner of my mind cleaned itself up and another corner of my heart started capturing bits and pieces of an old warrior's song. Buddy was the first to realize what was happening to me. We didn't talk about it, but I knew that he knew that through arranging this fishing trip he'd unknowingly thrown me a rope and pulled me from spiritual quicksand.

We caught bass that afternoon and evening the likes of which I'd not done in decades, not since my youth. We caught bass, fine bass in the two- to five-pound class, one after another, battling them to the boat, pulling back on our rods, reaching deep into the water and into our souls to link with a treasure that I'd just about given up for lost. The fishing put me back into a world where I belong . . . a world of water, of boats and fish and people who catch fish . . . in a part of the country that whispered my name and with people who speak a language I could understand.

The sun faded. We secured our gear in the boat, cranked up the outboard motor, and headed for the dock. The quiet purring of the motor, the shadows around and within the dock, the bumping of the boat against the wood, the creaking of the planks, the rattling of fishing rods and tackle boxes, the sloshing of iced-down fish in coolers, the way the vegetation crept from the shore out toward the dock, the crunch of gravel as we drove through the woods, back to the lodge, and then on to Poynor for supper at the crossroads café—all blended into an internal symphony that made me want to run to the top of a hill and fill the evening with a warrior's cry and song and then, like the cowboy on the ranch's archway, kneel in prayer, thanking God for good friends and good fishing.

As we entered the café at Poynor, there were greetings all around. We headed to the back of the place and into a room where there was a buffet and all the cold, sweet tea you could handle. The talk was good talk, rich talk, talk focused on fishing and dogs and guns and land and water. The waitresses kept those glasses of tea full and we kept the plates full . . . barbeque ribs, catfish fillets, vegetables cooked just right, jalapeno peppers all around, good spicy cornbread, and banana pudding.

We pulled away from the rustic little café after supper, with the echoes of the girls who spoke with a Southwestern twang still lingering in my mind. The turns in the hills back to the ranch, the call of whip-poor-wills as we pulled into the lodge, the deep bellow of bullfrogs resonating across the lake, the smell of open spaces, the sky so deep, the stars so bright . . . all this made me remember the story, a parable of sorts, that Buddy had shared with me earlier that day.

It was the tale of two loggers. One took a break every hour and the other just worked on through the day without resting. At the end of the day, the one who took the breaks always seemed to have cut more wood. When the other logger asked him how he managed to do this, the one who took the breaks said, "When I'm on my breaks, I'm sharpening my chain."

I realized that I'd been charging ahead, full-tilt boogy, for a long time, going hard at my work without sharpening my chain. And then I thought to myself, "I still have two more days to get that chain to a fine edge." I crawled into my bed that night with a smile on my face and a prayer of thanksgiving in my heart.

The next morning we fished the lower end of the big lake. There was an east wind and the fishing, while good, was a bit tougher. We fished harder and made up for it, shifting techniques, shifting gear, moving from plastic worms to top-water plugs, then to spinner baits, even fishing some for crappie and bluegill. I finally settled into using a small crank bait called a "shad-rap." It proved to be the magic combination. I fished it with my spinning rig and started hammering the bass. Buddy and Larry switched to similar lures and we were in business. One after another, those big Texas bass started coming to our boat and filling our ice chest. We kept all of the fish that we caught so that I could work them up later, getting data that would be used for a report back to Paul Calhoun. Buddy and Larry also wanted to take home some fish fillets. We were essentially the only anglers on the water, and our harvest was insignificant relative to the population of fish in that lake. In fact, as I looked at our catch, it became pretty clear to me that even though we were catching a lot of fine fish, the lake was, in fact, overpopulated and in need of a good thinning.

We stopped at midday for lunch back at the ranch's lodge. It was a light lunch but enough to dictate a siesta. Buddy and Larry flopped down on some overstuffed couches in the great room of the lodge. I walked out to a screened-in back porch with some huge hammock chairs that were hung from the porch ceiling. The wind drifted across the ranch, onto the porch, and into my soul. I closed my eyes, listening to the distant rattling of purple gallinules down on the lakeshore vegetation. I stretched, kicked off my boots, stretched again, and slipped off into never-never land . . . wandering across hills and beneath ancient walnut trees . . . talking with my grandmother on her front porch.

An hour or so later we collected ourselves and headed out with Paul to take a look at his ranch. It was obvious that he was fully aware of the blessing he'd received from his grandfather. He cherished the land and his connection to it. He drove across rangeland and down through bottoms and on into and through thickets. Here and there he'd stop and share his vision of what the land will become through his nurturing and dreams. And he spoke of the people he shared it with, the men and their families who also called the place home and who worked alongside him. They didn't work *for* him as much as with him, and, in fact, he'd even provided land and equipment for them to create their own movements within the symphony of land and water stewardship: a garden here and there . . . a few acres for truck crops . . . a home for an old fisherman who had held a special place in his grandfather's heart.

Then we went to another lake, a newer lake, one that was smaller ("small" is a relative term that must be applied in the framework of a Texas mindset) and had lots of standing dead timber and downed structure. Paul pulled into a parking area near another old covered boat dock and we all got out. Two well-used boats with trolling motors were tied up and waiting for us.

Paul and I took one boat. Buddy and Larry took the other one. And we fished. Lord, did we fish! I decided, however, that I'd fish for bluegill rather than bass. I'd brought along a tiny 2-weight fly rod for that purpose. It is really too light for bass and too precious to me to risk breaking while playing anything over a couple of pounds (or so I thought). It is my treasure, custom-built from fine blanks, with silver-nickel hardware and a handle made from the original walnut stock of my own grandfather's shotgun.

To minimize the chance of catching bass, I decided to rig up with a "bream-killer" fly rather than a popping bug. It didn't work. On my second cast, just beyond the boat dock, a four-pound bass nailed that bream killer. I saw the fish charging from a shallow area near a log and desperately tried to snatch the fly away from the monster. But the bass was too fast, and to my horror, I found myself solidly roped to it. My little rod arched. I tried to point the rod directly at the fish, hoping that it would break off. But I'd used the leader too much on past trips, and it had been trimmed back to where it was too strong to break. I had no choice . . . play that bass. And play I did. Never in my life have I had such a fight on a fly rod. That tiny little rod bucked and strained . . . and held. The bass went berserk time and time again, coming clear of the water, shaking its head, thrashing, taking hard, charging runs, and boring down on old logs and stumps. But finally, with the bass exhausted and me breathing a sigh of relief, I was able to lead the beast to the boat and net the thing. Although there was a cool breeze blowing, I had sweat all over my forehead.

After that bass, things settled down. I started catching bluegill, fine, fat bluegill with shoulders, and Paul kept bringing bass to the boat. We'd worked nearly the entire perimeter of the lake by the time the sun dipped below the hills. Then I got my nerve up again and switched to a popping bug. Almost immediately I was solidly hooked into another fine bass of about two pounds. My confidence in the rod was growing, and so I cast again and had another bass . . . then again . . . and another and another and another. Finally it got too dark to see where I was casting and I got fouled on an old stump. Paul eased me over to it and I unhooked the bug. We both knew that it was time to call it a day, so we headed back for the dock. Buddy and Larry were already there and were talking about supper.

The next day dawned clear and a little windy. Larry and I would fish together from one boat, and Buddy and Paul would fish together from the other boat. We moved out to the center of the smaller lake we'd fished the evening before and begin throwing crank baits. For about two hours we were virtually in a bass storm. They were not the same size as those of the previous ventures, but who is going to complain when a steady stream of one- and two-pound bass is coming to the boat. I caught bass until I couldn't see straight. Then in one fairly open area I caught a crappie. That did it. I needed a different pace. So I switched to a small ultralight spinning rod and wore those crappie out. They came out of the water like silver flecked jewels on emerald settings. In all of my work in fisheries around the world, I do not think I've ever found a fish more beautiful than a freshly caught crappie.

For a couple of hours I alternated between bass and crappie, depending on the type of water we fished. Open, fairly deep water was for crappie. As we moved into shallower water or along the shoreline, I fished for bass. The fish kept piling up in the ice chest we had in the boat. Rarely was there more than a minute or two when we didn't have a fish on our lines. And looking across the water, it seemed that Buddy and Paul were also thick into fish. We all started boating four- and five-pound bass with a matter-of-fact attitude, hardly missing a beat in our conversations. Anything less than four pounds just got swung into the boat without bothering to use a net. If they got off, it didn't matter. There would be another one behind the next stump. It was some of the most incredible bass fishing of my entire life. It was the kind of bass fishing that is better than the stuff you see on the outdoor TV channels. It was better than the stuff you read about in fishing magazines. It was better than any bass fishing I'd ever imagined. And the reason I was there was to try to figure out how to make it better. Lord! And if fishing on a Sunday is a sin, I'm doomed.

We took a lunch break back at the café in Poynor. This time we all ordered hamburgers the size of dinner plates and as thick as your fist. The glasses of iced tea were at least half-gallon glasses, and they stayed full the entire time . . . it didn't matter how much you drank. Those girls were right there, hovering around, making sure that nothing whatsoever at all was amiss.

After we finished lunch we went back to the boat dock to clean and process the fish. I measured them and took scale samples. Buddy recorded the length and sex of each fish. Paul and Larry kept the electric filleting knives humming. As we worked, a huge alligator, perhaps eleven or twelve feet long, cruised up to where we were working to check out what was for dinner. We made sure that it was fish guts and heads. At one point, while I was working, Buddy motioned to me to look out of the window of the old fish-cleaning shed. That big gator had perched himself right there on the bank beside me, not six feet away. His head was twice as big as a commode seat and his shoulders were as broad as an executive's desk in the Peabody Hotel back in Memphis. God but he was huge. Then he backed up a little and, with little more than a ripple, slipped back into the dark water of the lake.

The last evening, after fishing awhile with crankbaits and spinners, I focused on fishing with a top-water plug. I'd caught so many fish in the last two days that I really just wanted to see if I could get a big one to come all the way up and rip apart a plug. I wasn't disappointed. As long as we stayed out of the wind so that I could work the plug correctly, the bass slashed and slammed and hammered that plug. My rod stayed arched nearly constantly as I cranked those bass, one after another, into the boat. They just kept coming at my plug and I just kept cranking them back to me. Finally, worn out, I started to piddle. Larry was in about the same shape. We'd each cast and then work our lures, then just sit there in the boat talking about stuff. The sun set and whip-poor-wills started calling. Herons flew to their roosts. We drifted back toward the boat dock and I made just one more cast to straighten out some kinks in my line. The lure lay motionless beside a stump for perhaps a minute while I worked the tangle out. Then I reeled in the slack and gave the lure just one tiny, trembling quiver. The world exploded around it and I had another fine bass on the end of my line. He wasn't huge, just a tad shy of five pounds, but he was a beautiful fish. He jumped and dove and rattled his gills at me with his body halfway out of the water. I kept the pressure on and eventually got him into the boat. Buddy and Paul were over by the dock just watching the spectacle. It was the perfect ending to three perfect days of fishing.

It was dark thirty by the time we had the boats secured under the covered dock and all of our stuff loaded back into the trucks. Then we bobbed and weaved our way through the Texas thickets, headlights flashing, back to the lodge for a steak dinner. Paul was in charge of the steaks. Drinks were poured and the steaks sizzled on the grill. Bread was popped into the oven and salad was mixed. There was a glow in the room and a glow within us. There was a glow among us also . . . four fishermen who had just had three days of incredible fishing in an incredible place, sharing a final evening together.

I set up a microscope I'd brought along with me, mounted some scales from fish we'd caught and also scales from an old trophy bass from yesteryear. I showed everybody how to age the fish, and then we talked about where the bass fishing should go and how to get there. The steaks arrived. They were steaks prepared to the glory and honor of Texas . . . thick, juicy, and so tender you could almost cut them with a fork. Paul had done himself proud.

As we talked and laughed and shared our stories over the dinner table, I looked over at Buddy and saw him looking back at me, grinning. I grinned back and he nodded ever so slightly. Both of us knew that something very powerful had touched my life in the last three days and brought me back to order and peace and put me back onto solid ground, and . . . that the demons were gone. I looked back at Buddy and across the table at Paul and Larry as they continued with their wild storytelling and reflections, took a deep breath, and thought to myself, "With men like this in the world, and places like this, and fishing like this, life is good and things are going to be OK."

After supper I walked alone back to the guest lodge. As I was crossing the lawn I looked overhead at the heavens as they can be seen only in a remote part of Texas. The stars were brilliant. The Milky Way was as clear and as awesome as it had been back when I was a child in the Ozarks. I paused, looked overhead, and whispered a simple prayer of thanksgiving that so beautiful a night could be.

The next morning as I was packing my gear and getting ready to leave for the long drive across Texas, all of Louisiana, and most of Mississippi, I caught myself whistling. Whistling?! I hadn't done that for a very long time. It was then that I realized something. My chain was sharp again.

The Fine Art of Piddling

PIDDLING IS THE ART OF ENGAGING IN TRIVIA UNDER THE GUISE of industry. It requires proclamations of high order within which are nested a mosaic of seemingly insignificant activities. The trick is to be able to move from one activity to another in such a way as to imply great effort applied to a sense of direction (which there isn't). Farmers, mechanics, sailors, most husbands (eventually), and almost all hunters and fishermen over the age of fifty are typically pretty good at it. It is also important to stay gone from those who might question not only the activities engaged, but their worth in terms of socioeconomic advancement. Specialized tools are essential (e.g., shotguns of all gauges and actions, trucks, dogs of all sorts, custom-built fishing rods, handmade knives, an assortment of rifles and handguns, boats, canoes, pirogues, traps, packs, antique lures, hand-tied flies, chainsaws, and . . . you get the picture).

Piddling requires occasional tangible results. Old lawnmowers, jeeps, tractors, and outboard motors, lovingly stored down in the shed, eventually have to run, particularly if you think you need a new set of wrenches. There must be enough seasoned wood stacked to last most of the winter (you can split some of it later on . . . nobody is noticing now). Deer, ducks, and other game must occasionally be shot, brought home, and prepared for meals. Ditto for fish.

Hunting and fishing for trophies is extremely dangerous because tangible evidence that you were doing anything "worthwhile" is too rare. In this regard, I've found that I can typically avert questioning by supplying my family with two deer, twenty ducks, a dozen squirrels, and around a hundred pounds of fish each year. Once these goals are achieved, I have, in my own mind at least, full license to piddle. Outwardly, however, I *never* provide *any* evidence that this threshold has been achieved. Not only would it create tension in the ranks, it would probably preclude technological upgrades (e.g., purchases of new rifles, fishing tackle, "experimental" ammunition and archery equipment, seed for food plots, new puppies).

With each decade I've refined my ability to piddle around in the woods, on the water, out in my shed, under a tree (especially when working on my tractor), or on my farm. Piddling is not really a seasonal phenomena, but I tend to have the strongest propensity for it toward the end of the hunting season . . . after (as mentioned above) I've already put a deer or two in the freezer and have a few packages of squirrels and ducks and perhaps a rabbit or two added for variety. I'm set for the year in terms of roasts, ground meat, and the makings of squirrel fricasseed, smoked duck breasts, and hasenpfeffer. My focus shifts. Priorities change. I breathe deeply and listen to the sirens call from hidden pockets of the wild around me and the wild within me.

By this time in the hunting season I've become a better woodsman and hunter than I was early in the season. I'm better at reading the mood of the woods, the water, and the weather. I seem to shoot better, see better, hear better, and have faster reflexes. But the pressure is off. The hard-charging hunts of early season are now past. Although I may be shooting better, I find myself actually shooting less. It's a time when I'm inclined to take my old double gun and go poking around in the bushes, kicking brush piles to see if there's a rabbit inside. It's a time for slipping quietly along trails in the woods and along the creeks for squirrels . . . and letting most of them go after a successful stalk . . . or for checking to see if the salamanders are breeding in the ponds, or looking for "varmit" tracks in wet spots and trying to decide whether or not to crank up trapping this year, or for flushing woodcock from the hillside by the young pines where ground tends to stay soft and the wind is blocked. Basically, this is when I ramble around and get reacquainted with the land in very deep ways. With the leaves off the trees I can see the lay of the land better. But I *am* a hunter, and it is the hunting that draws me out into the wilds during fall and winter and into these piddling ventures.

The day will usually start in the dark, under the stars, with just the barest hint of light in the eastern sky. It is usually cold, with frost sparkling on the landscape. I'll park my truck, grab my gun and my cup of coffee, and slip through the main gate of my farm. I don't use a flashlight. I know every dip and curve along the faint dirt road that leads into my property. Sipping the last of my coffee, and occasionally pausing to look at a dark tree line or just at the sky, I feel transitions beginning to stir . . . transitions in the day, transitions in my heart and mind. By the time I get to the plank bridge that crosses my largest creek, the coffee will be about finished. I swig down the last gulp, then drift across my pasture to a little strip of oaks that line my western property line. I'll put some number 5 or number 6 shot in a barrel choked modified or full, and, depending on my mood and whether or not the deer season is still open, I'll load the other barrel either with buckshot or number 7½ shot.

It's only about a five- or six-minute walk from my gate, across the pasture, and to the woods. The drift across the pasture is a transition between worlds. But even so, even after I get to the woods, the transition typically is not complete, and I have to consciously and deliberately slow myself down to a hunter's pace.

I start my ramblings with a hunt for gray squirrels. They are usually the first critters to stir. If I'm quiet, and particularly if I start my hunt by hunkering down at the base of some tree for a while, there generally will be a squirrel or two scampering by in the predawn light. They dart as shadows along barren tree branches, silhouettes against a sky with the brightest stars still shining, hardly hesitating at all, and typically offering pretty tough shots. Sometimes, during those first predawn minutes, I'll see deer as they drift along the edge of the woods toward the honeysuckle thickets beyond my fence line. Most of the deer I let pass, but occasionally I'll take one.

I watch as the world shifts from a nighttime mode to a daytime mode. I hear the last of the owls and the whisper of wings from the morning's first ducks. Carolina wrens, tufted titmice, and various woodpeckers dominate the early morning woods. Later come the thrushes, the robins, juncos, towhees, blue jays, and cardinals. As the sun brushes the tops of the taller trees, the crows wheel by and occasionally a flock of geese will pass. Sometimes there are hawks, but hawks seem to be more active during midday than during early morning.

I'll sit at that first tree for a while, soaking it all in, trying to still the internal dialogue from the other world, trying to get in tune with the spirit of things, sometimes even trying to pray. If a squirrel shows itself nearby, I'll take the shot. If it is distant, I'll get up and stalk. I like the stalking best because it forces me to move very slowly and look very carefully at the world around me. I cannot afford to snap a twig, rustle leaves, or scrape branches. A gray squirrel has just about the sharpest eyes and ears in the woods. Spook one and it disappears forever. They are incredibly fine little game animals. Every one is a trophy to me . . . an indication that the hunter's spirit that has drifted into me from generations past can still make it all happen.

When I shoot a gray squirrel I have to carefully mark where it fell because they are hard to see on the ground and, in the leaves, are masters of escape if not well anchored by the shot. The tail usually gives away the location . . . but not always.

Afternoon piddling is different. If it is cloudy I tend to hunt alone . . . to capture the enchanting somberness of winter landscapes. If it is bright, I'll take the dogs. One is a retired retriever. The other is a curly-tailed "feist" that thinks it is a squirrel dog. The feist will cast back and forth in front of me (but, unfortunately, not too far out), while the retired dog will follow at my heels. The combination of the three of us shuffling through the woods precludes effective hunting for the most part, but occasionally the feist will tree a squirrel and I'll shoot it. If, however, I had to depend on that dog, I'd starve. She *thinks* she's a hunter. Reality is something else . . .

But the other reality is that it doesn't matter. We're out there together enjoying the day, exploring the land, checking on frog eggs in the pond, looking for late-season buck rubs, crawling under barbed-wire fences and over levees to see if there are ducks on my neighbors' ponds (there usually are), watching hawks soaring with sun on their wings in a sky so deep that I'm convinced, if given a choice in reincarnation, I'd choose to be a redtail hawk, looking for cardinals in cedar trees, searching out the warm sunny spots that have the year's first wild violets, and quietly slipping through the shallows of a flooded spot in my pasture looking for fairy shrimp and clam shrimp . . . scratching a naturalist's itch.

On these late winter ventures, with duck season drawing to an end, I think about wrapping the season up with an afternoon duck hunt . . . but I invariably decide against it. Ducks need to know that they have a safe place to roost at night. I won't be the one to deny them this security.

As the southern winds bring spring to the landscape, my piddling intensifies but in a different mode. There is a strong focus on my fishing pond, and I am, after all, professionally, a fisheries biologist. My pond is only a shade larger than an acre, and because it does double duty as a duck pond, it is fairly shallow. As a result, it warms early in the spring, and with the warming comes the spawning and the fishing. I start with bass fishing, then switch to redear sunfish, then to bluegill, then . . . as spring becomes advanced . . . switch back to the bass. My bass fishing is with spinning tackle. My "bream" fishing is with fly tackle. I keep the pond slightly crowded with bass so that the bass will help me structure the bluegill population. The bass predation thins the bluegill population and the surviving bluegill grow exceptionally well. The bass, however, tend to be stunted. It's the tradeoff. Rarely do I catch a bass larger than two pounds, but the bluegill tend to be huge (greater than ten inches long).

So I piddle around with the bass, keeping those I catch (all sizes) until I see that their bellies are starting to get rounded. Then I quit fishing for bass until October. I need their help with the bluegill . . . to keep the spawning in check. And bluegill will keep on spawning in my part of Mississippi until October.

I fish for bluegill primarily with tiny weighted flies that I tie myself using fox squirrel and gray squirrel hair and wood duck feathers . . . all from critters I've shot on my farm. The flies that I tie are not very eloquent, but the bluegill don't seem to care. There is absolute magic when I'm catching ten-inch bluegill, one after another, on a tiny 2-weight fly rod. I have, in fact, frequently been late to church because I've said, "Just one more fish," . . . and ten fish later I'm still fishing!

Mid-summer piddling is, without a doubt, the most challenging for me. The older I get the more I struggle with hot weather. Subsequently, mid-summer piddling tends to be done on a tractor, early morning or late evening, mowing trails and the pond levee, disking food plots for deer, plowing fields to plant with wheat for doves and geese, checking on the milkweed (for monarch butterflies) and thistle (for goldfinches) and protected corners reserved for autumn wildflowers. I keep my pickup truck parked in the shade with a cooler of ice water and, occasionally, a couple of iced-down beers. Sometimes I take a rifle and a few targets and spend an afternoon "sighting in" even though the rifles really don't need it . . . they've been sighted in already, but I tell myself that things can change . . . powder gets old, scopes may have been inadvertently hit by a hard object (while resting secured in the cabinets), or I may have developed a different "sight picture" that must be adjusted for. It's all just an excuse to shoot and it really does increase self-confidence . . . important for any hunter.

When I'm not on the tractor I'm with a chainsaw cutting wood for the winter or trimming back the buttonbush in the duck pond so that I'll have an open hole for shooting once the duck season begins. If by chance I'm on the farm at sunset, I'll open my truck doors, turn on a country-western station, crank up the volume, and set off the coyotes. The coyotes on my farm truly love "honky-tonk" music. The music will drift across my pastures and the coyotes will join right in with it.

As the summer progresses, young hawks start hunting on their own. I love to watch them, especially the redtail hawks. I save a few corners of fields for them. Cotton rats will congregate in these corners, and, if I'll mow correctly in strips, it gives the young hawks open spots to nab a rat from time to time. Once while I was mowing strips, one of the hawks showed up. He'd sit patiently in the top of a tree beside the pasture, watching me mow. I'd mow a strip and out would come the rats. The hawk would nail them, then go back to its perch to wait for me to mow another strip. We teamed up this way for the better part of an hour and it seemed that he got a rat with every pass I made. As fun as such amusements might be, however, hurricanes are really the only saving grace for late summer . . . as long as they are no stronger than a category one or two. They're quite magnificent really.

August then mercifully rolls into September, and when it does my blood starts to sparkle again. By the second week of September there's usually a little cool snap that brings hope surging across the land and into my heart. The dusty dove hunts are winding down; teal and early Canada goose seasons are underway. Archery season starts the first of October and that requires practicing nearly every afternoon with the bow. In desperation I cook off the last of the venison burger and squirrels so that there won't be questions regarding the *need* for replenishing the stock in the freezer. I come bearing gifts to non-hunting friends and neighbors, making sure that none of the packages of meat have dates on them, but advising any and all that wild game is best cooked *soon*. My department head at the university reminds me that I have a job . . . at least for now . . . but by then it is too late. I am back on the front lines again, watching roofs for the season's first frost, listening for the haunting calls of wild geese at 2:00 a.m. And, as I mentally go through my piddling repertoire, making lists of things to do, the thought comes to my mind that I don't really have time anymore for a real job . . . I've got too much to do. There are owls out in my woods that I need to listen to . . . carefully. There are persimmon trees to check on. Some of them may require a deer stand. My guns need cleaned (again). My duck boat needs a new coat of no-gloss varnish. The mole salamanders will be out, on their way to the breeding ponds, with the coming of the first, hard, cool autumn rain, and I'll have to be in the woods with a flashlight to witness it. And of course there's fall fishing just getting cranked up, raccoon traps to blacken and lubricate, and I think that the cardinal flowers may just be coming into bloom . . . I should check on them. And the rains from the last hurricane probably scoured new fossils from the clay beds along the creek . . . I need to go see . . . before they're washed away.

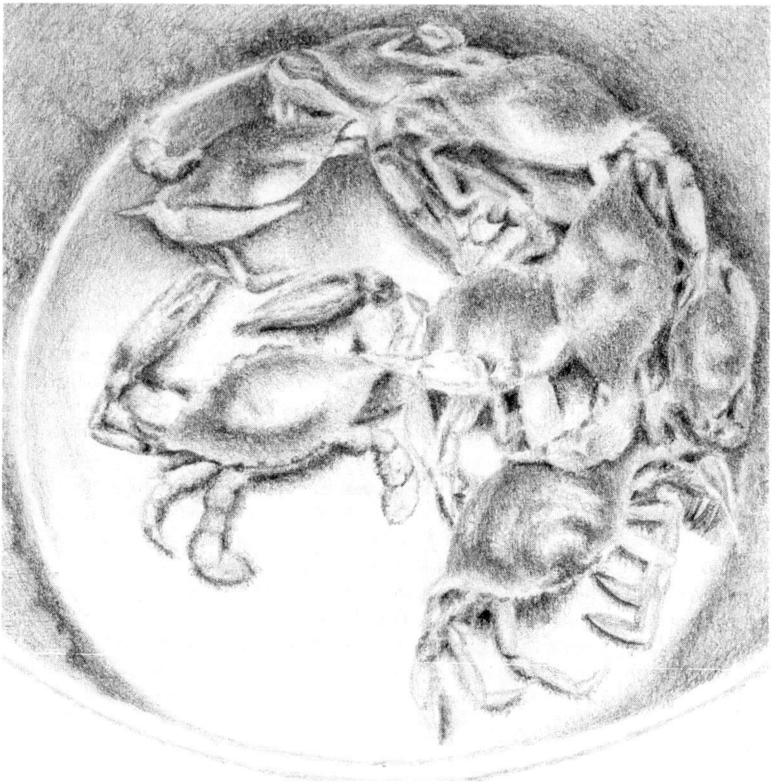

Rendering Southern Glue

The smell of the Pascagoula River marsh hung heavy in the thick August air as I backed my boat down the public ramp and into the brown-stained water. My daughter, Anna, held the bow line. Once the boat cleared the trailer and was floating, she leaned on the line and guided the boat alongside the wharf. When she signaled, "All clear!" I pulled the trailer out of the water and found a parking spot among the other pickup trucks and trailers, secured our rig, and walked back over to Anna and the boat.

We were surrounded by a world that has captivated us both over the past several years as we engaged in a father-daughter pilgrimage to the Mississippi Gulf Coast to go crabbing. Near the ramp there was a weather-beaten and rickety bait shop where ice, hooks, line, weights, frozen bait shrimp, and live bull minnows were for sale. Just beyond the boat ramp was a small harbor where a small fleet of shrimp boats was moored. Further out a menhaden boat was weaving its way along a channel on its way to the fish-processing plant. A few gulls wheeled lazily overhead. A small flock of brown pelicans glided on stiff wings just above the water's surface. Mullet dimpled the still water. It was good to be in this salty world and especially so with my daughter.

As Anna steadied the boat I loaded our crabbing gear and an ice chest. After putting on life jackets we crawled into the boat and took our seats . . . Anna in the bow and me in the stern. Then I cranked the

10-horsepower outboard motor. Although the boat was over fifty years old, the outboard motor was new. It started easily and settled quickly into a very quiet, very smooth purring. Slowly I backed away from the wharf, shifted into forward gear, and moved the boat out into the little back bay that led to the marsh.

For the first half mile or so we were sheltered from wind by a peninsula that led out to a bridge spanning the channel. But as we motored under the bridge there was a slight chop to the water and a flapping ponytail. Anna looked back at me with a huge grin all over her face. This is her element! How she loves it!

My little boat is made for such water. It is twelve feet long with a rounded bottom and a good, high, V-shaped bow that cuts through small waves like a dream. It is an old boat, but as solid and as tight as they come. Back when it was made, manufacturers used very heavy gage aluminum to build boats and built them to last a lifetime . . . which it has. It is a bay boat, a marsh boat, not a river boat. It has high gunnels near the bow in order to cut the waves, and then it tapers gracefully toward the stern. The beam is fairly narrow so that it can slip through channels and into tiny pockets of the marsh. But in spite of that, it is incredibly stable. Once anchored in a crabbing hole, or when fishing, a gray-bearded papa and a ponytailed young un' can get up and move around it in without worrying too much about tipping.

On we went, beyond the bridge, beyond one of the Pascagoula River's channels, and out into the marsh. The tide was falling, exposing mud along the base of the *Spartina* grass fields that blanketed the higher ground. Old, long-dead snags jutted up here and there and served as perches for ospreys that prowled the area. On the muddy banks all manner of small shorebirds swarmed. Herons and egrets stalked the shallows searching for small fish and crustaceans. As we rounded one bend, a small alligator, perhaps four feet long, cruised along with only its head and snout showing. When we came closer it submerged with a big splash and swirl.

Anna sat in the front seat, with spray occasionally drifting over her as we went through larger waves. This world of salt marshes is perhaps the one best in synchrony with the beating of her heart. She loves the wind in her hair and the spray in her face. She loves the mud flats and the critters that scurry across them. She loves the big sky full of sunshine and the open water that shimmers like a mirror or sparkles like jewels. Although I was driving the boat out to the crabbing hole, I wasn't the only pilot onboard. Anna has been driving boats since she was ten years old and is very good at it. She has the cool head of a young lady who knows her stuff. Not only is she an accomplished small craft pilot, she was, at age thirteen, also an experienced outdoorswoman, at home in wild places, and she knows her first aid. I couldn't have been in safer hands or in better company. On top of it all, there is incredible magic in the world when you share it through the senses and perspectives of a thirteen-year-old girl. All I had to do was let her guide my focus.

It took us about twenty minutes to get to the crabbing hole. It is tucked back away from the main channel around a couple of small bends where a tidal creek has scoured the bottom a bit deeper. It is sheltered from wind by the *Spartina* grass and from waves by the bends in the creek. It is probably somewhere around a hundred feet long and perhaps half as wide. It absolutely oozes mystery.

We dropped anchor and prepared our crabbing gear . . . such as it was. Basically, all it consisted of was two twenty-five-foot-long pieces of cotton twine, each with a lead weight on the end. Near the weight we tied on a raw chicken leg. The other end of each line was tied to a support inside our boat. We threw the chicken legs out as far as we could and let them sink to the bottom. Then we opened the ice chest, grabbed cold drinks, and settled into our surroundings . . . waiting for crabs.

It wasn't long before one of the lines began to tighten and move. Anna carefully began pulling it toward the boat. I got the long-handled dip net. As is almost always the case, the crab tugging on the end of Anna's line would not turn loose of the chicken leg. Eventually we were able to see it, hanging on tightly, twirling its back legs, trying to swim away. My job was to get the net under it without the crab seeing the net and then scoop it up.

Anna and I are a well-oiled "crabbing" team, and in short order Mr. Blue Crab was in the boat. I grabbed it out of the net, quickly measured it to be sure that it was of legal size, and then plopped it into the ice chest to mix with our cans of cold drinks. We shut the lid of the ice chest and for a few moments could hear the crab crawling around inside. However, within a couple of minutes, after cooling some on the ice, it stopped its scurrying and all was still.

The next crab came quickly, but as I was trying to get it out of the net, it hung momentarily on the net by one of its claws and then dropped into the bottom of the boat. It crawled off quickly into a corner and went into defensive posture, with both of its big claws held high and ready for a fight.

The trick to capturing a crab like this is to come at it from behind and grab it tightly. It will try to reach back to get you, but *generally* the claws are too short to do that. Remember that I said *generally*.

Crabs can see very well. They turn to watch you trying to come from behind. So I usually put one hand in front of the crab, make some motion with it, and then, while the crab is distracted, make a quick snatch with my other hand from behind. Timing is everything. Done poorly, the crab will have you rather than you having the crab. But this time, I won and the crab joined his buddy in the ice chest.

The afternoon deepened and the crabs piled up in our ice chest. We needed a lot of them because that evening we were invited to a crab boil at a nearby hunting camp. Anna and I mostly sat quietly in the boat, occasionally sipping on our cold drinks and connecting with the beauty of the marsh.

The entire mixture thickened. Thunderheads billowed in the sky around us, with streamers of light shooting around them as the late afternoon sun found openings to shine through. Terns and gulls wheeled and darted, occasionally dipping into the water for a small baitfish. Occasionally a large commercial fishing boat would pass by out in the channel, rumbling and churning, creating a wake that would gently rock our boat, even tucked back into our little hideaway as we were. Otherwise, the quiet enveloped us, broken only by an occasional shifting of position on the boat seats or the popping of a top from a can of cool drink. We didn't talk much, just an occasional comment about the wind or the water . . . or to announce that there was a crab on one of the lines . . . or to share a thought about how all that was around us fit together and how we were also part of it all.

More than those occasional passages would have broken the spell that the marsh and the crabbing had cast on us. Crabbing is, after all, one of those precious activities where you discover (once again) that it is perfectly alright for two people to sit in a boat and focus on filling an ice chest with crabs and filling hearts with a beautiful sense of contentment that lets you know that there isn't much in the world that could possibly be more important than what you're doing out there, at that moment, in that boat.

Crabbing is something that you can do without interrupting your train of thought or whatever conversation you may be having with your partner. When your partner is your teenaged daughter, the gift that is crabbing becomes precious. Whatever is said in the boat stays in the boat. Dreams can rush into the clouds of never-never land. Big questions can be asked and answered. Disappointments and challenges can be discussed. You talk if you want to or stay quiet if you want to. You are surrounded on the inside by an oversoul, establishing a sense of separate peace, and on the outside by a sanctuary composed of earth, wind, sky, water, and life so thick that it is almost overwhelming. And all the while you are gluing the component parts together by slowly pulling crabs into the boat.

Just before sunset we took stock of our catch and declared that we had enough for the evening's crab boil. The wind had died and the entire marsh was as still as a church sanctuary on a Monday morning. Anna pulled up our anchor and I cranked the little outboard motor. We putted out of our hidden spot in the creek and out into the main open-water channel of the marsh. The sun and clouds were perfectly reflected in the still water. I increased the throttle of the outboard motor and we sliced our way back to the bridge and the ramp without so much as a bump. It was gorgeous, all golden green mixed with brown water and azure sky.

Once back at the ramp, I got the truck and boat trailer, backed the trailer down the ramp, and held it steady as Anna drove the boat up onto the trailer. I winched the boat tight, made sure that everything was straight and balanced, and, with Anna still onboard, pulled the rig up the ramp and out into the parking area. The only folks around were a few fishermen who had just come for an evening of stalking redfish and another group gathered alongside the shoreline, fishing for whatever might bite.

After securing the boat, we drove about fifteen minutes to a hunting camp just outside of town where we met my friend Linwood Grierson. Linwood, a lifelong resident of the area, was an officer with the Mississippi Wildlife Federation. It was through the federation that we'd originally connected, and it was Linwood who actually introduced me to the mystery, magic, and incredible fishing to be had in the Pascagoula marsh.

When we got to the camp, Linwood helped us clean the crabs and then fired up the cooker. A few of his local buddies then arrived and good fellowship ensued. There was cold beer for the grownups and cold pop for the kids. Twilight drifted on the landscape and the talk and fellowship became ever richer. There was an indescribable sense of connectedness among us . . . sons and daughters of the South . . . young and old . . . visiting, joking, poking at the boiling crabs, going time and again to the coolers for drinks, letting the power of Southern communion with the sacraments of friendships, tall tales, and spicy, boiled crabs pull us ever closer together.

To be sure, the South is replete with "glues" like this. All of the glues require some sort of sojourn into the wilds or out on the water, preferably with a compadre or two (young un's are best) to collect essential ingredients . . . including, of course, stories about the ventures and the people who made them. These glues ultimately take the form of clam bakes, oyster roasts, fish fries, crawfish boils, and even "wild coon" suppers (I'm not aware that there *is* another sort of "coon" other than "wild" . . . but for some reason they are always called wild coons for these suppers) or squirrel or quail dinners. But for me, when I want to plunge into the deepest currents of Southern culture, I'll do boiled crabs out in some camp with my friends and my daughter down on the Mississippi coast. When all the ingredients are right, and stirred together in the proper way, as they inevitably are, I have yet to find a stronger glue.

Bristle-Face Cathedral

The hush was so thick in the predawn darkness that even the occasional sound of a paddle bumping against the side of the boat in front of me seemed to be sucked right out of the air. Pillars of tupelo gum and cypress towered around me, reaching up toward the heavens as starlight cast its magic on the still waters. I didn't want or need another light as I navigated my canoe among the trees and on into the open area beyond them where decoys would be set for a morning duck hunt. My companions spoke only in whispers. Their whispers and long periods of silence acknowledged reverence for our surroundings. Although unspoken, there also were prayers of thanksgiving for places like this and for opportunities to be in them.

Such is the power of Bristle-Face Cathedral, the vast, flooded forest that surrounds a huge beaver swamp near Greenwood, Mississippi. It is a fitting name for the place because it truly is a cathedral in every sense of the word. When you're in the place there can be no doubt regarding the presence and power of God. And . . . it is prowled by duck hunters who hunt with a very special breed of bristle-faced dogs.

My canoe was loaded with gear for the hunt, and on top of it all perched one of those bristle-faced dogs named Beauregard. His running buddy, Hatch, was cut from the same mould and sat on a similar pile of gear in the other boat. This would be my second day of hunting ducks with American Wirehaired Pointing Griffons. Their owner, Guy Ray, a longtime resident of the Delta region of western Mississippi and eastern Arkansas, led our little caravan through the watery cathedral, paddling his tiny metal duck kayak to and through an obscured opening in buttonbush and on into the duck shooting hole. Don Flynn, a lifelong friend of mine from Hot Springs, Arkansas, and John Lee, a seasoned hunter, leader in waterfowl conservation, and resident of Greenwood, Mississippi, were in the other boat.

A cold front had moved across Mississippi the previous afternoon, bringing with it cooler temperatures and, hopefully, new ducks to the region. The hunting had been good the previous day, with mallards and gadwalls coming regularly to our decoys. This time, however, with the northwest wind that followed the front, and because ducks land *into* the wind, we'd have to hunt on the other side of the open area among the bushes in order to keep the wind to our back. We were hoping for the best but uncertain about how the new conditions would affect our hunting.

Setting up with our backs to the northwest wind would be a little tricky. Although not particularly critical during the early minutes of the hunt, it would force us to face into the sun after sunrise. Camouflaging the boats and ourselves was absolutely essential. A shiny gun or a hunter's face, or even an uncovered wet paddle reflecting light could cause the ducks to flare before coming into shotgun range. Equally as important, for hunters and dogs, was remaining very, very still . . . especially as ducks circled our decoys, trying to determine if it was safe to come on in.

After the decoys were put out and the boats were shoved back into brush and covered with old strips of cotton burlap, we took our positions. Each dog had his spot in the canoe and settled in. Each hunter found a tree or a clump of thick brush to help break up his outline.

Unlike the previous day, there were few ducks flying at first light. We could hear them in the distance and occasionally saw small groups passing high overhead, but none really seemed to notice our decoys, and only a couple gave us a quick pass-by within range . . . and they were on us and gone before we realized it. Twenty minutes into the hunt we only had three ducks among us . . . one mallard and two gadwalls.

Just as sunrise started brushing the tops of trees, lots of ducks started flying. But they all seemed to prefer a place some four hundred yards away to the west. They'd give our decoys a little scrutiny, circle once or twice halfheartedly, then drift off to that other place, cup their wings at great altitude, glide in seemingly forever, and land with their buddies. Once on the water they were essentially down for the count, and odds against us were compounded. It's hard to compete with a wad of live ducks on the water.

We settled into waiting, filling the moments with discussions about dogs and guns and ducks and conservation . . . listening to and watching virtually thousands of snow geese pass high overhead and fade into the distance . . . occasionally seeing a duck that seemed interested in landing someplace and doing our best to lure the rascal to our decoys with seductive calls. Sunlight flooded our shooting hole and we had to move into the shadows of trees in order to stay hidden.

Then, perhaps forty minutes or so after sunrise, ducks began working our little area. They'd come over in small groups of five or six, as singles and as pairs. Most were gadwalls, but there also were prized mallards. The green heads of the mallard drakes would glisten in the sunlight. The white underside of wings would flash. We could hear the whistle of wind against stiff pinions.

The ducks would circle and circle and we'd call, pleading with them to come on in and join all those fine, peaceful ducks that had a secure resting area in the hole that stretched before us. With each pass they'd lose altitude and then . . . finally . . . there would be a moment of intense quiet . . . the ducks would lock their wings, drifting on whispering air. As if they had minds of their own, shotguns suddenly would be up and ducks would fold, hitting the water with hard splashes. Some stayed where they hit. Others, however, would quickly regain their sense of position and, with great flapping or with heads low to the water in a sneaking strategy, do whatever they could to put distance between themselves and us.

On command the dogs would be out of the canoe and into the cold water, surging toward the ducks, instinctively knowing that they had to deal with the cripples first. Often both the dogs and the ducks would disappear from sight and all we would be able to hear was thrashing out in the water. This sent messages of drama unfolding beyond us, echoing through the eons of time as dogs became extensions of human hunters, accomplishing what no person could do, instinctively knowing how to use wind and cover to find and capture prey, and then, bound by some invisible thread of love or loyalty or respect or perhaps all of these, securing the game for the hunter, and, in the case of ducks, bringing it back to the hunter's hand. There is a bonding, a synergism, that links dog to hunter and hunter to dog that is immeasurable and beautiful beyond recounting. It exists in dimensions beyond the mind . . . transcending even dimensions of the heart. It defies words, but it fills us with a sense of rightness. There's something in it all that tells us that, at least during these moments, the world is as it is meant to be.

The dogs would come back to us, ducks secure, sometimes still very much alive, and deliver them to Guy's hand. Then they would launch themselves from water two feet deep and land back in the canoe . . . back in their positions . . . ready for the next round. The dogs received praise from us all and they seemed to appreciate it. But I watched them closely and sensed that the praise really wasn't necessary. They were born to do what they were doing. Once they were back in their positions in the canoe, they almost immediately began casting their eyes to the horizons, looking for more ducks, intent, intense, and seemingly feeling complete . . . just as were their human companions.

After an hour or so, with several more ducks added to the growing bag in the canoe, a shifting of feet by hunters and more frequent talk among us sent a signal that the hunt was winding down. There were feeble attempts to move out toward the decoys to start picking them up and to retrieve the empty shotgun shells that were floating around us. But then, inevitably, another group of ducks would swing by and we'd be in the duck shooting business again. Finally we took tally and found that we had thirteen ducks: seven gadwall, five mallards, and a black duck . . . one duck beyond half a limit . . . and for all of us more than enough to stroke our hunter's hearts with satisfaction, a dimension of being that transcends happiness, absolutely.

It only took us a few minutes to gather our decoys and other gear, pull the boats from their hiding places, and start the journey back to our launching point at the edge of the swamp. As we left the openness of the buttonbush zone and entered the realm of towering trees and reflections in Bristle-Face Cathedral, we were once again stilled by an almost overpowering sense of sacredness.

There, on the still waters of the cathedral, I found myself drifting more than paddling, trying to hold on to the hunt, to life in the present tense, and to the place for as long as possible. I found myself for a few moments deep in reflection . . . and in prayer . . . quietly focused on the beauty that surrounded us and the treasures of our hunt: the precision and poetry of wild ducks in the winter sky, the companionship of fellow hunters, the artistry of a good spread of decoys, the wonderful dogs doing outstanding work, the fluid synchrony of a hunter and his gun that results in a good shot, the unspoken anticipation of duck dinners with good friends and colleagues, the rich yet fragile heritage treasured by sportsmen, and especially the heritage of duck hunters and duck hunting . . . and the longing, so deeply held in our hunter's hearts, to pass it all along to future generations . . . with all the parts intact.

Postscript: I bought a bristle-face puppy and named him Hank. Beauregard and Hatch are his cousins. As I write this, he is one year old. He knows basic field commands, is an obsessive retriever, and holds steady on points. He's become my rambling buddy and has captured my heart.

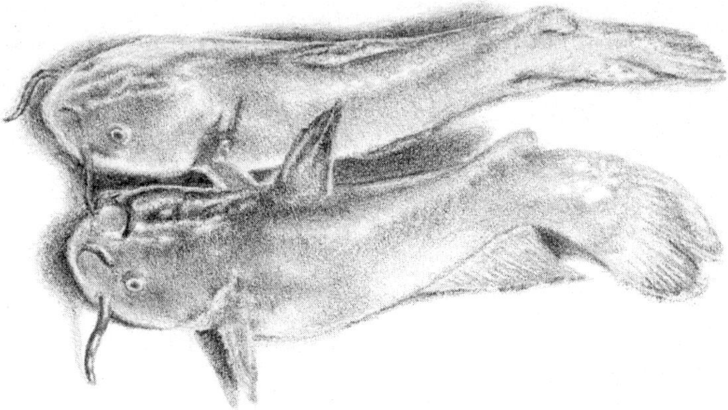

Mud Cat Connections

TWILIGHT SETTLED GENTLY ON THE HILLS AND MY HEART AS I parked my vintage station wagon on the remnants of what once had been a section of the main highway linking Northwest Arkansas with the Arkansas River valley to the south. The curve in the old road, however, had been too sharp, and so a new, broader, and safer curve had been constructed, leaving the old section to settle into the earth.

The edges of the old road's pavement were now irregular and overgrown with vegetation. Grass grew up through the cracks. But it was still a solid place to park and, with the sharp curve and a thick stand of oak and hickory that lined it, this little section of history provided perfect cover for a fisherman who didn't want passing cars out on the main road to get the idea that there was something of value in the area. Only a few local folks and Ozarks woods ramblers like me knew about the gravel lane connection between the old and new road. The connecting lane had been discretely established by a landowner so that he could get to the gate of his property. There was no marker.

Full of peace and with a night full of promise wrapping itself around me, I gathered my gear. It didn't amount to very much . . . just a battle-scarred spinning rod with an equally scratched-up reel full of ten-pound test line, a gas lantern, and a five-gallon bucket. The bucket held bait, a few hooks, and a cord stringer. The bucket would serve as my seat as well as a way to carry back my catch. The stringer was to keep fish fresh and alive while I was still fishing.

Ozark streams have fine reputations as places to fish for bass, trout, and walleye. But on this evening my focus was on something entirely different. I was after mud cats. However, in the stream I was going to fish, such a name really didn't fit because the stream was clear and the bottom was primarily rock and gravel. The more correct name for this group of fish is bullhead catfish.

There are three main species of bullhead catfish: black, brown, and yellow. They are small catfish, rarely weighing more than a pound, with a reputation as hardy, opportunistic fish that can live in small backwaters where environmental conditions can become at times a bit challenging. In ponds, sloughs, and oxbows they are known to bury themselves in bottom ooze when these places dry seasonally or during drought. They stay hunkered down in their little cocoons down in the mud in a state of aestivation, waiting until conditions improve. Add water and, bingo, you've got fish again. In streams, they will congregate in residual pools as flows subside during summer.

Without the influence of predation, populations of bullheads can become overcrowded and very stunted. But in places where there are predatory fish like bass to keep the pressure on them, bullheads can become a really nice size. Once cleaned, they fit perfectly in a frying pan. They are very good fish on a dinner plate; and in fact, in my opinion, they can be the best catfish there is in that regard.

I'd fallen in love with bullheads when, as a child, I'd fished for them in Kentucky stock ponds during my father's seminary days. Later, after we'd moved to Central Arkansas to kick off his post-graduate career in ministry, I fished for them in small creeks. There was something sort of special about bullheads, especially the ones in creeks. I knew that they were wild fish. Hatcheries didn't stock bullheads, and typically they didn't stock creeks. Although I certainly enjoyed fishing for bass and other sunfish and even larger catfish like channel catfish in a collection of small lakes near my home during my teen years, the magic of wild fish, and particularly bullheads, drew me ever closer to their haunts in streams. When I moved to Northwest Arkansas for my university studies, bullheads and moving water continued to cast their spells on me . . . spells that have been enduring over the decades.

On this particular evening, as I collected my gear, crossed a barbed-wire fence, and started down the slope of a rocky pasture to the stream at the bottom of the hill, my plan was to fish one of the stream's residual pools that I'd found on previous ramblings. Although I hadn't fished for bullheads on this particular stream before, I knew from some of my university field studies that it had bullheads and also that it had its fair share of bass . . . enough to keep bullhead populations in check. So I decided I'd give it a whirl. My target would be black bullhead, the species that tends to be most common in upland streams.

The stream was about half a mile from where I'd parked the car. As I walked in the ever-deepening evening, the stars began to pop out in the clear mountain air. I could hear the calls of night birds: screech owls, chuck-wills-widows, and occasionally a barred owl. There were also calls from various frogs, mostly cricket frogs and bullfrogs. I wasn't in any sort of hurry. If there was going to be bullhead fishing that night, it would only improve as the night progressed.

I didn't use the lantern as I walked. There was enough light from the stars to guide my way. Ahead of me I could see the dark outline of trees that lined the stream, and I knew from previous squirrel hunts along the stream that there was a little break in that tree line that would guide me down to the water. Beyond the pasture and that tree line I could see the surrounding hills. I took a deep breath and felt a surge of happiness course through me. It is a world that I love, one that fits me very well.

Passing through the break in the tree line, I dropped down into the stream's channel. There was only just a little current trickling across shelves of flat limestone outcroppings and through gravel bars that in other times of the year would be riffles and rapids. I sloshed and slid my way downstream, keeping to dry rock as much as I could but not avoiding direct routes through shallow water. There was a slight chill to the air, but it was not uncomfortable.

It wasn't long, perhaps ten minutes at most, before I got to the place where I wanted to fish. The stream slipped across a gentle staircase of rock outcroppings and then made a sharp bend to the right. Opposite from the staircase was a steep bank. The pool between the staircase and that bank was about a seventy-five feet wide and perhaps two hundred feet long. I estimated the depth of the pool out in its deepest parts to be around six to eight feet deep, certainly not more. There was a wall of forest on both sides of the stream, but out there on that rocky staircase I had plenty of room to move around and enough space for my bucket and lantern and for casting.

Setting my gear down on a broad rock shelf next to the water, I dug into my shirt pocket for matches. Then I pumped the fuel tank of the lantern, struck the match on my pants zipper, and, holding the tiny flame close to the lantern's single mantle, turned the lantern's valve until fuel began flowing. The mantle quickly caught the flame and I adjusted the fuel until I had a strong, steady light. Once adjusted, the lantern made a soft, hissing sound that only seemed to intensify the awesome quiet that surrounded me. The world contracted to the small circle of light cast by the lantern. The shadows were deep, but I could see well enough to make my casts out into the pool.

Searching in the circle of light, I found a piece of driftwood about as big around as my arm and two feet long. I placed it close to the lantern and then, reaching into my bucket, put the bait next to the wood. I would be using beef liver as bait tonight and the driftwood would be my cutting board.

Next I rigged up my rod and line. I tied on a strong 4/0 hook with a short shank. There was no perceptible current in the pool, and the weight of the bait would be enough for me to make my casts. So I didn't add any additional weight to the line. After my casts, the bait would drift slowly down to the bottom; and, with the unweighted line, I'd be able to tell immediately when fish were on my bait. After securing the hook to the line, I carved off a hunk of liver about as big as the end of my thumb, threaded the bait onto my hook, flipped the bucket upside down, cast out into the pool, and settled down on my seat.

I love the sweet feeling of being alone out there in the night, with the stream, the night birds, the frogs, the trees, and the mountains. I love the quiet, with only the faint tinkle of a tiny little trickle of water moving over the rock staircase and the soft hissing of my lantern. I love the way that life transitions from day to night in these Ozark streams, with aquatic insects emerging from the water to complete their life cycles and little catfish starting to stir down in the dark depths of the pool. The insects, once beyond their aquatic nurseries, flew in circles around my lantern. I knew that the catfish were stirring because I could see little tugs on my line.

Finally, after a minute or two, one of those little tugs shifted into a slow, steady pull. I could see my line start to tighten. When it was perfectly straight I snatched back on my rod. Out on the end of the line I could feel the fish twisting and pulling. It wasn't the flash and dash sort of fight that comes from bass and trout but rather a good, solid, deliberate pull. Slowly I reeled in the fish. As it came closer to the rocky ledge I could see it splash in the light of the lantern. When I got it up next to the rock where I was stationed, I simply lifted it from the water with my rod and swung it around behind me, up next to the lantern.

It was a fine bullhead, about twelve inches long, and probably weighed about half a pound. It moved its pectoral spines back and forth, making low, resonating sounds. Its broad head and smooth, scaleless body glistened faintly in the light as it wriggled and squirmed up on the rock shelf. I laid down my rod and went to it. Picking it up carefully in order to avoid the two sharp pectoral spines on its sides and the equally sharp dorsal spine on the top, I pulled the hook out from the corner of its mouth. I checked the color of its whiskers beneath its mouth and, finding them dark, confirmed that this was a black bullhead. Then, still holding it carefully, I got my stringer and punched the sharp end through the bottom of the fish's mouth from the outside and threaded the cord out through the mouth. On the opposite end of the stringer was a metal ring through which I looped the stringer's point in order to secure the fish to the line. This would be my "anchor" fish. All other fish would simply be strung on the line on top of this anchor fish, without any sort of additional tying.

I found a crack in the rocks near the water and shoved the stringer's point down into that crack. Then I pitched the fish, now secured on the stringer, back into the water. It swam out to the end of the stringer's cord and quickly settled down, seemingly accepting its fate.

I baited my hook again, cast back out into the pool, and settled back down on my bucket seat. Two minutes later, I had another bullhead on my line. This fish set the pattern of the night. I moved deeply into it, casting, hooking, retrieving fish, stringing them, settling back on my seat, time and time again. My thoughts drifted deeply and were not interrupted by the fishing or the fish. Such is the magic and the beauty of bullhead fishing on a summer's night in the Ozarks.

I wasn't wearing a watch and, in fact, during that chapter of my life, as a young man fresh back from two years overseas as a US Peace Corps volunteer, I didn't even own a watch. So I had little idea of what time it was and it really didn't matter. I was where I wanted to be, doing what was right and natural. There was no schedule. The only goal was communion with the mysteries of life lived in the present tense out there under the stars on the bank of that stream. I'd leave the stream when I had enough bullheads on the stringer, although I had not defined "enough." I'd know it when it happened . . . but reality suggested that it would probably be defined by the amount of bait I'd brought with me.

The fishing was good, but it was the night that held me. The light from my lantern played on the water and on the riparian forest, with shadows that danced with a cadence all their own. The pool was the home of beaver, and for a while I watched as a mother beaver with her kits moved downstream and eventually crawled out on a sandbar that melted into the darkness. A water snake was attracted by my light and I had to gently push it away and back into the water with a stick. Upset by the encounter, it had released its pungent odor, and for a while the smell hung heavily in the still night air. Then there was a long period of quiescence . . . and with it came the thoughts of a solitary man on a single-lane track, with most of his life yet before him. I breathed consciously and purposefully, drawing in the essence of earth, wind, and water. The frogs had stopped calling and the evening chill had slowed the chirping of crickets. The owls were going about their business and didn't have time to call, hoot, trill, or growl. They were searching for their prey in a quieter way, just as I was . . . but their prey had fur or feathers. My prey was ethereal vision and dream.

A persistent splashing down by my fish stringer brought me to attention and I refocused on the more tangible, physical world around me. The splashing continued. I got up, walked down to the water's edge, and discovered that the water snake I'd messed with earlier was trying to eat one of my smaller bullheads. I tried to push him away with a stick, but he was committed to his task and wouldn't let go. So I reached down, grabbed him behind the head, lifted him from the water, and pried his mouth from around my fish. I told the snake that I was a fan of opportunism but would not cotton to the ways of a thief. He would not be allowed to steal my fish. He would have to go catch his own. Later, however, I sort of felt sorry for that old snake. I had plenty of fish and I sure could have made his evening more pleasant by giving him a free lunch. There's nothing wrong with helping a snake, even those who tend not to express higher degrees of gentlemanly temperament (and water snakes fall into that category!).

The snake encounter was enough to resurrect my fishing. I reeled in my line and found that the hook was bare. There was no way to know how long that bare hook had been out there in the pool. It could have been half an hour or it could have been two hours or perhaps more. I couldn't recall when I'd last made a cast because the entire venture to and on this stream that evening had been defined by wrinkles in time. But the wrinkles, rather than the angling moments, had taken me where I wanted to go.

That's actually what fishing is really all about anyway. It is a way to be out doing something "practical," to use Joseph Conrad's frame of reference as stated by the ex-patriot butterfly collector in *Lord Jim* . . . something practical that only sets the framework for endeavors of a higher order. But those endeavors take time to evolve, and for me, they take solitude and wild places . . . space around me and within me. To achieve their fullness, I need days on a trail or in a canoe. I must be where the winds of the soul can blow freely. A couple of weeks tend to do it. But for periodic reinforcement, an occasional night out fishing for mud cats on an Ozark stream works very well.

Through such endeavors I am able to plot my course for the chapters yet ahead, evaluate situations, and resurrect great music (which in my mind I can actually "hear"). I engage in very personal discussions with the old masters, the early church fathers and theologians, the ancient ones of cultures, thought, and the arts East and West, and, in the resulting dreamtime, work collaboratively with them to shine lights on the common denominators of shared human pilgrimages . . . the eternal truths of humankind that transcend temporal and spatial dimensions. Ralph Waldo Emerson called this realm of being the "oversoul" . . . the realm within which humankind reaches out to touch the hand of God that has been extended to us. That hand is always there; we only have to reach out to it. And if we don't reach far enough, God's hand comes ever closer. Sometimes we don't have sense enough to reach at all, and that is when God surely must take a deep breath and sigh before going the full distance to come all the way to us . . . to take our hand when we don't even know that we need it.

The lantern sputtered. I pumped its tank a little to brighten the glow. Then, turning to my bait can, I realized that my bait was gone. I may have used it fishing. Just as likely, it was pilfered by other night critters out on the prowl while I was in my dreamtime. Regardless, it was time to wrap up the evening, an evening that in and of itself had been a prayer. Just being there was a prayer. No words had been expressed. They were not needed. The communications were far beyond their containment.

The fish were still on my stringer (the snake was finally gone), and they only splashed a little as I picked up the stringer and deposited the entire catch, perhaps eight or nine fish . . . I didn't count them . . . into my bucket. Then I turned off the lantern and stood there in the dark.

From a practical perspective, it is best to walk with a cool lantern to avoid burning thighs during a trek back along the creek and up the hill to the car. But from a different perspective, within a different dimension, standing still as the lantern cooled, with a chill that was not of the night winds coursing through me, I realized that waiting just a bit for the lantern to cool had something else of value on this night full of mystery and practicality. Sharing my breaths with something beyond myself, I raised my face to the heavens.

The stars can be awesome on an Ozark night.

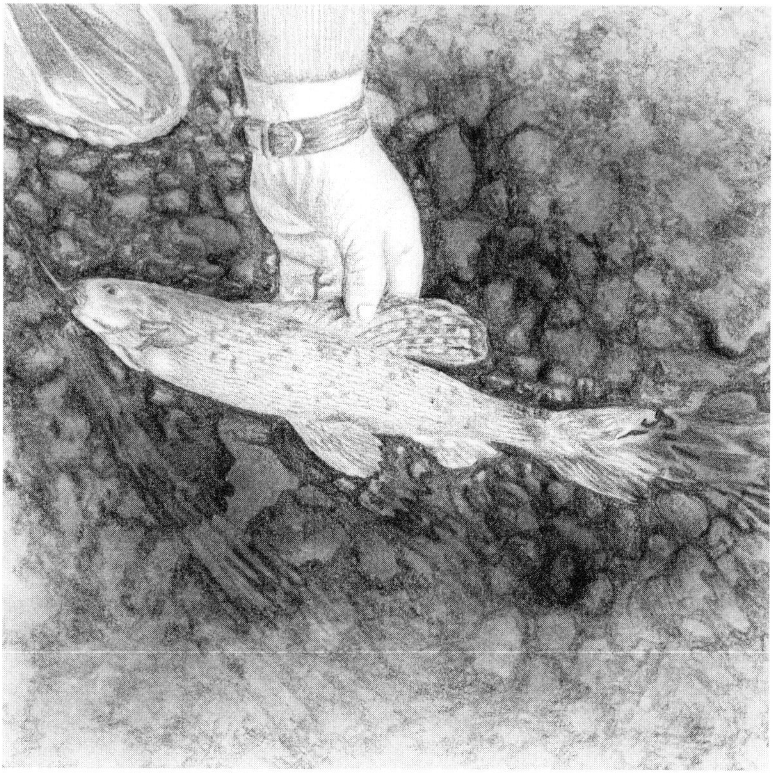

Before Winter Comes

AUTUMN WAS FADING FAST IN NORTHEAST ALASKA. I STOOD alone in the middle of it all, caught up in the changing of the seasons . . . amid the vastness and the magnificence of the far northland that has owned my heart for most of my life, feeling a damp chill creeping up from the icy Coleen River and a dry chill slipping down from the Brooks Range mountains that surrounded me . . . alone out on an ageing snow field, a vestige from the previous winter that lingered on here after the brief arctic summer, a legacy from the past as well as a reminder of things to come . . . enraptured by sky and mountains and valleys . . . just listening . . . opening myself up to messages that drifted from the landscape.

As I stood there, the afternoon sunlight searched for openings in the clouds and, when finding one, created shafts of light that produced a flow of golden luster and emerald shadow that moved among the red- and gray-tinged mountains and valleys. There was an incredible stillness . . . a stillness with so much power in it that I could feel its grip tightening around me, binding me, bonding me again to the arctic.

It was as if the entire region was taking one final, deep breath before winter. And, as I stood there, caught in moments of vespers,

I reflected on my own seasons, passages through a mortal sojourn, and began to realize that in all likelihood I, too, was taking one final, deep breath of remote Alaska before moving into *my* winter. For more than thirty years, since age twenty-six, I'd been coming to these northern lands. Coming, leaving, coming again, leaving again. I'd tried to stay, every time, searching for a way, any way . . . but responsibilities beyond Alaska, professional as well as personal, always pulled me back to the "outside."

I sensed that at the age of fifty-seven this trip could be and most likely *would be* my very last *deep* venture into Alaska wilderness, at least a venture of the drop-off variety where a small plane leaves you several hundred miles away from anything that could come to your aid in case of "special circumstances." Yes, this probably would be the last time I'd watch a bush plane become a tiny dot in the sky, then follow it on and on, more with the mind than with eyes, and, finally, realize that it had long ago vanished from sight . . . leaving me beside a lake or on a strip of tundra or gravel, with my small pile of gear and a very special feeling of loneliness that I've treasured all of my life.

Some things, like the very last meeting with a loved one or the very last time spent in a loved place, you just know. There's a dimension of awareness telling you that this is in all likelihood *the last time.* It comes from somewhere beyond the heart. It intensifies the experience. Everything seems to be in sharper focus. The colors, even pastel colors, seem more vibrant. The sounds, the smells, the senses of touch, the senses of feeling, the senses of the soul—all are set on their edge. You cling to all that is around you but without some forced, gaudy exhibition. It is precious beyond treasure and you know it. And, as I searched my heart and soul for guidance in the face of this reality, I found no sadness in the reality that I was ageing and probably would never venture this way again in the arctic. Rather, as I stood there surrounded by the wind and the mountains, there was incredible strength that came from understanding and accepting that I'd done things right . . . at the right time . . . in the right places . . . and that from such ventures along life's pilgrimage a man moves on . . . following dreams and the meditations of his heart until the last breath is drawn and released.

I cherished where I was and what I was doing. I knew that this trip to arctic Alaska would be a real battery charger for me. Most importantly, however, I knew that it would help take me, well prepared, into the winter of my mortality. Then, with the fullness of heart that comes to me when I'm where I belong, doing what I should be doing, I took a deep breath, straightened, stretched, and turned from my vespers to continue my trek across the snowfield.

I was carrying a very special, custom-made 2-weight Sage fly rod (with the handle made from my grandfather Jackson's old shotgun stock) in my left hand, a fly box full of nymphs and dry flies of several patterns and sizes in my coat pocket, and a .44 magnum revolver on my belt. The revolver was loaded with heavy bullets (in case of a bear emergency), but I also had a few shot cartridges for it in my coat pocket in case I stumbled across some ptarmigan for the pot.

After about fifteen minutes of rambling I came to the edge of the snowfield, carefully slipped down from it to the river, and began sloshing alongside and across the river's braided channels. I was searching for something more substantial than the shallows I found in these braided channels. I was searching for deeper pockets and runs and pools where arctic grayling likely would be lurking.

Finally, after a half an hour or so of rambling, ahead of me, from along a distant rocky bluff, I could hear the faint but steady rushing of bigger water. Even from so far away it seemed to overwhelm the tinkling and slosh of shallow water over riffles and the crunch of gravel under my boots. I think, however, that it was really more a matter of focus.

I'd locked my focus on the sound of big water and it became the most important sound in the entire world. It was my siren's call. If I could get to that main channel, I knew that I'd find the grayling I was seeking.

But getting to the big water was an incredible challenge. I had to work myself through a maze of braided channels that are so typical of arctic rivers. It was like solving a puzzle with no obvious solution. Many times I had to back track as I became trapped by flows that, while not sufficient in depth and other habitat features for grayling, were nevertheless still deeper than my knee boots could ford.

There were several hours of daylight remaining and, since everything was in good order back in my camp, I'd dedicated the afternoon to exploration of the Coleen's headwaters, and to fishing. I could take my time and solve the puzzle of how to get to the big water. There was no need to rush. In fact, rushing would have been exactly the opposite of what needed to happen in my heart and soul. There was mystery. There was beauty. There were discoveries to be made. It was like making love to a beautiful woman. Never rush. To rush is not God's design. The present tense is too precious.

I slowed down . . . and so did time. I think that was the secret that closed the gates to one world and opened those of another to me.

At that moment a raven called my name and a gentle north wind brushed my face. There was magic in that wind. It caused a stirring within me that sharpened my senses. It connected me to the rich earth smell of Alaska. It helped me see the world around me with the resolution of a voyager. I focused on vistas and passes and grand patterns of the land at a scale that matched that of wilderness . . . an entire mountain range rather than a hillside, the sweep of a valley rather than a rockslide or burn, hundreds of square miles rather than forty-acre blocks, a complete river, including its entire drainage, rather than a portion of the river's main channel.

My stride and pace changed. They shifted to a mile-eating flow that engulfed the "outside" world tendency to pick my way cautiously along a track. I let my legs and feet do their own thinking . . . and was reminded again, remembered again, with amazement, that they could still do it and do it very well. I tuned my hearing to transcend the ringing in my ears that is the product of too many shots fired with big guns. I was, in fact, transformed back to a more original, purer state of being . . . reconstituting, becoming, once again, the man who for millennia traversed this and similar landscapes throughout the world. THIS has always been my reason for returning to Alaska . . . not the hunting or the fishing, or other general outdoor ventures. I come to Alaska to become man again.

About twenty minutes later I found myself on a small spit of a gravel bar alongside the main river channel. The water was rushing tight below a rocky bluff. There were a few large boulders scattered in the channel that created eddies and resting places for grayling. My heart was beating hard and my spirit was soaring as I slowly moved into position for casting.

It had been much too long since I'd last fished for grayling. They, beyond all other northern fishes, hold a special place in my heart. It was grayling that I angled for during my very first venture to Alaska, back when my beard was black and testosterone surged in my blood. During that summer (1977) I'd traveled with a companion for days and then weeks into remote backcountry, with an eighty-pound pack on my back, a hickory staff in my right hand, and some fishing gear to probe the streams. I didn't find much fishing water in the high, glacial region of the Alaska Range where I traveled, but when I did it was wonderful. Grayling captured my heart then and have held it ever since.

I'd been told that on this section of the Coleen River it was best to use the smallest black dry fly I could find. I had several tied on number 18 and number 20 hooks. I'd also been told to expect grayling between six and twelve inches long. But, with the fast current in this main channel of the Coleen River, coupled with my lack of faith in being able to fish the tiny dry fly in this fast water, I selected a larger black nymph. It was tied on a number 12 hook.

The water was fast but extremely clear. The day was slightly overcast, with only occasional periods when the sun would send streamers of light drifting across the valley. I wasn't worried too much about spooking fish with my shadow. I was more concerned with drag from my line and an unnatural drift of the nymph.

I played out some line and began working into my cast, back and forth, back and forth, perpendicular to the direction of the stream flow, until I had what I thought I needed, and then let the nymph settle about six feet above a boulder, below which was a big eddy. As the nymph moved past the eddy, I saw a twitch in the line and pulled back. I was hooked to something solid. Then I realized that

I had a fish on. My little rod bowed and all I could do was hang on. Then, there was slack. The fly had pulled out without me ever getting a look at the fish.

I reeled in my line, checked my fly, and then, working the rod and line back and forth several times, I again got the distance I needed to lay the nymph back across the current so that it could drift into the eddy. Just as the nymph passed the boulder, I got another strike, and this time I knew for certain that I had a fish on.

The grayling took off downstream and then turned into the current. I couldn't get it to move so just hung on . . . keeping the pressure on it, but being careful not to pull so hard that I'd pull out the hook. After nearly a minute of holding position, the fish started moving again. I played line in and out, letting the little 2-weight rod keep the pressure on the fish. After about another minute of fighting the fish, I got my first glimpse of it. It was a beautiful grayling.

I could see it clearly in the emerald green water. It had its huge dorsal fin fully erect and was using it to its advantage in the current. Then it jumped. I lowered the rod tip immediately to keep the fish from smashing the fragile tippet that I had tied to the nymph. Two more jumps and one more dart into the current and the fish began to tire. I worked it into shallow water and gently slid my left hand under it, lifting it from the water.

It was splendid. It was gorgeous. The forecast for this river having six- to twelve-inch grayling had been incorrect. This grayling I'd just caught was every bit of eighteen inches long and probably weighed nearly two pounds. The steely gray sides merged with the faintest of pink that seemed to intensify, only slightly, however, near the gill operculum. The dorsal fin, fully erect, was iridescent with incredible spots. I held the fish gently but firmly and removed the hook. Then I slipped it back into the river and watched it swim slowly back into the dark eddy.

Over the course of the next hour I caught and released another seventeen grayling from that pool. The smallest was fourteen inches long and the largest pushed eighteen inches. I was beside myself. The rushing water, the arch of my little rod, the chill in the air, and those gorgeous and incredibly strong fish filled my heart to the bursting point. Between fish, I'd just stand and look at the water and the bluff and the gravel bar I was standing on. All the elements came together into a perfect blend.

But eventually I wore out my welcome. After several unproductive casts and drifts, I realized that I'd educated these fish. It was time to move on.

I backtracked across the braided channels to the edge of the river and then continued moving upstream. I walked for over two hours and probably four or five miles without locating anything that looked remotely like the grayling water I'd experienced back along that rocky bluff. So I climbed up onto a cut bank to get some elevation and a vantage point and to survey the landscape and perhaps locate another pool.

Just below the cut bank I was standing on was a little run of slick water that seemed pretty shallow at first glance. But as I watched I saw a slight swirl in the water. It caught my attention and I waited to see if another would come. It did. There were fish in this little run. It was perhaps thirty feet wide and maybe a hundred yards long. Although most of it seemed too shallow for grayling, next to the bank the water was a little darker and a little deeper.

I climbed down from the bank, crossed over a riffle below the run, and positioned myself on the gravel bar across from the cut bank. The dimples and swirls I could see on the slick surface of the water were very small. Accordingly, I figured that the fish also were small. So I decided to try one of those tiny black dry flies that had been recommended. The eye of the hook on that tiny fly was so small that I could barely get the 5X tippet (about 2-pound test) through it.

I cast across the current and a little upstream from where I'd seen one of the swirls. The tiny fly was tough to follow. Then, suddenly, there was a slight dimple and splash and I realized that I was fast to a fish. And it was not a small fish! It had all the power of those I'd caught from the first pool. But here the current was not so strong and so the fish did not have that extra help.

I landed the grayling in fairly short order. It was a fine fifteen-inch fish. I decided to keep it for supper so quickly killed it and placed it into a tiny, isolated pool of cool water that was nearby on the gravel bar. I checked my fly. It was still in good shape, so I cast again. Almost immediately I had another fine grayling jumping on the end of my line. It was a wonderful fish, full of strength and determination. It plunged as deeply as it could into its pool and then made a solid run upstream. I worked it gently, keeping pressure on it, but not forcing it. Eventually it tired and I was able to slide it onto the gravel bar. It was another nice fish approximately fifteen inches long. I quickly killed it and placed it beside the first fish I'd caught from the pool. That was enough for supper.

But I kept on fishing . . . catching and releasing at least a dozen more fish over the course of the next two hours. Those grayling loved that tiny black dry fly. They averaged somewhat smaller than those in the first pool but were still fine fish. My smallest fish was twelve inches long. My largest one was the first one I'd caught. I loved the way they'd take that fly. Sometimes they'd barely dimple the water and suddenly the fly would be gone and my line would tighten. At other times, they came up with a slight splash as they hit the fly.

Then, finally, as the fishing began to wane, I stopped. I'd fished enough for a day. The pool was exhausted. It was getting late into the afternoon. It was time for me to start my return to camp.

I reeled in my line, took off my fly, and, for a while, simply stood there. I looked around me at the river, at the gravel bar, at the mountains, at the sky . . . breathing slowly and deeply the damp arctic air . . . feeling the power of being the man I really am, in the place that will always be home to me. Walking over to the little pool where I'd placed my two grayling, I picked them up, carefully placed them in my shoulder satchel, pulled my revolver out of its holster to check the loads, put it back, adjusted my satchel across my back, took another deep breath, looked around again, and began the three-hour walk back to camp.

My transformation was nearing completion. I knew it. Alaska once again was working its magic on me, penetrating to the core of my being. There was purity of thought and clarity of vision that only comes to me in this place. I could feel it. It was so deep. I took about ten more steps and then stopped and looked around me again. The Alaskan stillness was all around me . . . and within me. Power surged through my body. Taking another deep breath, I felt the power surge through me once more. I was whole again. It was good to be home.

I sloshed through a shallow channel, crunching my way along the gravel bar, and climbed up and across an elevated gravel deposit and through a small stand of alders growing along the main riverbank. A ptarmigan chattered in the waning light. A hawk flew overhead; distant peaks were full of shadow but still had sunlight brushing their tops. The river sang to me.

Beyond the alders I crossed a mud bar. The bar had fresh tracks of caribou, moose, and bear . . . wilderness wanderers, like myself, marking their passages as seasons shifted in the arctic. Their tracks were joined by tracks of the man.

I moved steadily on toward my camp as dusk deepened into twilight. As the last light faded and the night's chill settled on the land, I quickened my pace . . . but just a little. There really was no need to rush. Passage under starlight was as beautiful as it had been under sunlight. I knew the way to camp. I've known it since the beginning. And I knew . . . I knew . . . I still had miles to go . . . before my winter comes . . . and all of them are precious.

Forgotten Reaches

THERE WERE ECHOES FROM A RIVER PAST AS OUR TWO CANOES slipped into the cool, clear waters of the White River upstream from its confluence with the Norfork River in the Ozark Highlands of North Arkansas. The echoes came as whispers on the dawn wind. I could sense them, deep and stirring, as fog swirled above the waters.

Although it was a Sunday morning and the peak of the summer tourist season, we had the river to ourselves. My older son, Robert, steadied the canoe we'd share as I took my position in the stern. My younger son, David, was already in the other canoe with a friend of mine from Louisiana, Nelson Ball. Robert was on summer break from college. David, a high school student, was in the middle of his second year as an apprentice fishing guide on the river. Nelson was in the Ozarks on a mission of reconnecting with land he owns not far from the river.

For two days we'd fished for rainbow trout in the river's reaches twenty miles or so below the Norfork River confluence. We'd caught a few fish, but the fishing was challenged by a plague of floating moss clumps that fouled our hooks on nearly every cast. I'd fished for trout in the river for decades and had never encountered moss like that before. Rumor had it that it was an exotic species that had been accidentally introduced into the river by an angler who wore waders he'd used while on a trip in the western United States. Rumor also had it that the moss in the reaches of the White where we'd been fishing actually came from the Norfork and that upstream from the confluence fishing on the White was pretty clean.

From the riverside fishing resort where we were staying, just north of the town of Mountain View, a boat ride that far upstream was pretty much out of the question. However, the resort owner and longtime friend of mine from boyhood, Joe Peceny, said that he had canoes we could use and would be glad to shuttle them for us to those upper reaches. We figured it was worth the try and that even if the fishing wasn't good, we'd have a good float trip down a scenic section of the White.

The upper and middle reaches of the White River in northern Arkansas and southern Missouri have long been world renown for float fishing. Long, shallow-draft, flat-bottom boats used on the river were designed to drift slowly downstream as anglers cast into the pools and riffles that coursed through some of the prettiest hardwood hills in the country. Because the river etches its path across a region rich in limestone, biological productivity at all levels along the food chain was and continues to be very high. Historically, there have been lots of fish for the catching, and generally some big ones too. In this regard and prior to the mid 1900s, the river was especially famous for its smallmouth bass fishing. Then came the dams.

The lakes behind the dams filled with clear, clean, nutrient-rich water. During winter, they chilled down, *way* down. In summer only the top layers of the lakes warmed up. The bottom layers stayed cold and, because of the clear water, light was able to penetrate deeply into the lower strata. As a result, cold-water "wintertime" plankton were able survive and flourish throughout the hot southern summertime. The plankton produced high concentrations of dissolved oxygen in these deeper layers of the lakes.

The dams were designed to produce electricity for the region, so, to ensure a dependable source of energy, the generators pull water from as deep in the lakes as possible. Releasing this cold water from the bottom of the lakes downstream into the tailwaters below the dams shifted the biological dynamics of these stream reaches. Even though there were lots of nutrients in the water and plenty of oxygen, the water was simply too cold during the spawning season for native fishes such as smallmouth bass to be very successful, and also too cold for many of the aquatic invertebrates that historically sustained the native fish populations.

Within a few years, and because of the cold water, sport fish populations in the tailwater reaches below the hydroelectric dams declined to almost nothing. The fisheries and the tourism associated with float fishing on the rivers languished. Recognizing responsibility for loss of the river fisheries as a result of the dams, the federal government built trout hatcheries and stocked the trout they produced, as well as coldwater invertebrates to feed them, into the tailwaters. Local people quickly adapted to the new fish and the new conditions on the river. The tourist industry rebounded to unprecedented levels as the surrounding region capitalized on the magic and mystique of trout fishing and framed it in the history, culture, and beauty of the Ozarks.

Although there are several dams and tailwater trout fisheries along the White River as it courses through the Ozarks, the section of the river where I've always fished for trout starts below Bull

Shoals Dam near the Arkansas-Missouri border and continues for about 150 miles downstream. However, as the river flows downstream it warms and, during summer, by the time you get to the confluence with the Norfork River it is almost too warm for trout. Then the shot of cold water from Norfork Dam knocks the temperature of the White River back down to the point where good trout waters continue for another 50 miles or so downstream.

Anglers on the system, local as well as tourist, tend to have a fixation on trout. Other fish don't matter very much to most of them. So they generally fish the upper reaches of the White River below Bull Shoals Dam and then sort of fade away the further you get from the dam, just like the trout they fish for. By the time you get down to the town of Calico Rock near the Norfork River confluence, there's almost nobody at all on the river. Then, the trout fishing cranks up again, beginning on the Norfork River below Norfork Dam and continuing on downstream to and on into the White River.

As we paddled out into the currents, echoes from the old river of pre-dam days grew stronger and stronger and filled me with their haunting chorus. There was a rich smell coming from the water, the wet rocks, and the forest. It triggered something within me, creating wrinkles in time, reconnecting me in an almost seamless way with days I'd spent on the river across the years. They all blended into one, in dimensions beyond time. I shut my eyes momentarily. I could hear a gentle rush of water against rocks. I opened my eyes again. A great blue heron on a water-soaked log stood motionless until we were within a few feet of it and then squawked and flew off with heavy wing beats. The surrounding hills were covered by a soft blanket of green forest, broken here and there by limestone bluffs. Our paddles made gurgling sounds as they moved through the water alongside our canoes. Water slipped beneath us with a quiet rush. The sounds, the visions, the sense of belonging created a stillness within me that intensified the echoes from the old river.

We could occasionally see fish dimpling the water's surface out in the channel and knew these to be trout. But closer to the shore and around submerged logs and rocks we could see other fish . . . smallmouth bass as well as other native fishes such as suckers, sculpins, and smaller sunfishes. And, very importantly, as we peered down into the water, there was no moss drifting in the currents. This was a blessing. We would be able to fish without fouling our hooks on the stuff that had plagued us the previous days.

We waited until we'd paddled through the first set of shoals just below the launching spot before we started fishing. Then, almost immediately, we started catching fish. After the first few we could quickly tell whether the fish on our lines were trout or bass, even before seeing the fish. The trout would twist and flash and move seemingly at random. The bass, on the other hand, would slam our lures and then rip away line as they headed for cover.

Within the first hour we'd each caught over a dozen fish and on average had caught two or three bass for every trout caught. The trout fishing was good, but the bass fishing was fantastic. Most of the trout were between ten and fourteen inches long. We were able to get them into the canoes fairly quickly, and just as quickly we unhooked and released them. Although they were fine fish, they didn't seem to have much fight to them in the warmer water. The smallmouth bass, on the other hand, were in their element. They fought with all their heart and muscle, sometimes jumping, but always putting a strain on our light tackle. They were full-bodied fish in excellent condition. Although most of the bass weighed around a pound, we caught some over two pounds, which, on ultralight spinning gear, will keep the juices flowing in just about any angler. They had a glare in their eyes and were full of fighting spirit as we unhooked them. When released back into the river they almost always went with a hard splash.

After a couple of hours of fishing we learned how to reduce the trout catch and stick with the bass. There was simply no question as to which fish we wanted. I saw this evolution especially strong with Robert. His pace of casting slowed. There were fewer random casts. He was picking his targets and working his lure deep into the hidden pockets. The bass rewarded him accordingly.

Robert is an artist and a quiet young man by nature. But as that wonderful morning on the river progressed, and his fishing became more focused, I'd hear an occasional quiet laugh as he'd set the hook or a soft exclamation, "Ha!" . . . "All RIGHT!" . . . "Wow!" as one of those brown bass cleared the water and then went ripping away, with Robert holding on tightly, little rod bowed, line ripping off the reel. Once he had his fish in the canoe, there would be the look of triumph on his face. Then, with the look of triumph transforming into a look of peace, he'd gently slip the fish back into the river, watch it swim away, and look around at the river and the hills . . . ever the artist, the reflective man, capturing the essence of a precious moment on his pilgrimage. There might be better experiences for a father to share with a son, but I'm not sure what they possibly could be.

About mid-morning we stopped on a gravel bar to rest, stretch our legs, and explore some. David, the adventurer, was almost immediately in the cool water, swimming and splashing, diving and drifting in the current. Nelson and I watched him for a while, a young man full of energy and spirit, connecting fully and directly with the river's currents, and then we drifted away down the gravel bar, rambling along the water's edge, looking at deer and turkey tracks. Robert poked around backwater pools watching the little fish, mostly minnows and darters and a few sculpins, dart among the gravel and then joined his brother for some swimming in the river. All around us was the magnificence of an Ozark morning . . . woodpeckers calling, squirrels barking, crows cawing, and hawks screaming. There were a few turtles basking on logs. The sun flashed on the riffles below us. A gentle breeze moved across the waters.

It was only then that we saw other people on the river. Like us, they were in canoes. But they were not fishing. They were just drifting and enjoying the tranquility and beauty of river and hills and forests and critters. We only waved. To have spoken would have broken the spell for us all. Then they were gone, leaving us with a sense of sweet loneliness that somehow was made more intense by the encounter. Sometimes you have to lose something, like solitude, even if only for a few moments, to understand better its significance, its value, its treasure.

We gave the folks in the canoes time to move a few bends downstream from us before we launched ourselves again into the currents. The sun was coming across the hilltops now and the fog lingered only in the protected hollows. We had no schedule to keep and no purpose other than to live in the present tense. And we moved ever deeper into it, pausing to look at particularly interesting rocks jutting out into the stream, sometimes putting rod and paddle aside and just letting the currents carry us into the dreamtime, watching the fish deep in the clear water, among jumbles of boulders and old waterlogged trunks. The rapids brought joy and sparkle into the moments as we felt their currents tug on our canoes and felt their splash on our faces. And then we'd fish some more.

The further we drifted downstream, the better the fishing got. There were ever fewer trout and ever more bass. With the sun higher in the sky, their bronze sides seemed almost golden at times. And as they came from the water, still full of fight, they glistened like precious jewels . . . which they were. And, because jewels tend to lose their brilliance when removed from their setting, we released every single one of them.

Although it remained unspoken among us, and each of us no doubt had different words for it, it seemed that all of us recognized that as we moved along that section of river, with the hills calling our names and beckoning us to stay . . . if only a little longer . . . that our real reason for being there became ever more clear. We'd come for trout fishing and fun, and a little bit of adventure. But then a shift occurred.

The remnants of the old river enveloped us. We were immersed that morning in solitude and beauty and a sense of connectedness . . . with the hills, with the currents, with each other . . . with existence beyond time. The river's echoes pulled us ever deeper into the realms of being beyond the physical and used the magic catalyst of wild smallmouth bass to overwhelm us, to humble us . . . with the river's awesome message of power and resilience. It was made clear to us that the old river is *not* gone. It is not a river past. It does not exist only in the memories of old men. It is still there with all the essentials required for resurrection.

That section of the White is a seed from which the river in its fullness of being will ultimately sprout and triumph again. The dams will eventually crumble. The exotics, the transients, those who do not belong there will go away and leave the river to restore itself. Our civilization will fade and be transformed into something that we probably cannot even imagine. Through and beyond these passages, the river's echoes, those deep haunting echoes that reverberated that morning on the river and continue to reverberate in my soul, will prevail. The bass that now lurk within the White River's forgotten reaches will rise from the shadows in triumph and proclaim their sovereignty, their rightful position as princes of the waters.

Generations from now, on a still morning, as fog swirls among the hills and birds call and hawks drift along limestone bluffs and the currents ripple and glide, the river will itself hear an echo from the past . . . the echo of my genes drifting up as a song through the heart of an angler I will never know, as a line tightens and clear water explodes in golden fury. I think I can hear that angler's song echoing faintly but clearly across the eons of time . . . and it fills me with incredible peace.

Vesper Bridges

In the cemetery behind a rural Kentucky church, a tiny rock pool in the shadows of huge maples dimples as striders dart upon its surface. I see the reflection of a boy's smooth face, my own, and then peer deeper into the pool, hardly breathing, heart beating so hard in expectation of an encounter, searching for any trace of the leopard frog that jumped into the water at my approach. More than anything in the world, I wanted to hold that frog in my hands, not as a predator, not as a captor, but rather as a way of linking myself to a world beyond my own, a world of life where I could not live as a boy, and where, ultimately, the frog also could not live . . . but it could stay in it longer than I could. On previous trips to the pool, I'd plunged my face into the cool water, holding my breath as long as I could, opening my eyes, trying to see through the blur that clouds vision when a being seeks entry into a different medium. Although I couldn't articulate it, capturing the frog, holding it in my hands, would bridge the worlds, bridge realms of being. I understood sacrament . . . the bridges . . . before I could define it.

Finally, I saw a slight movement under a leaf, lunged forward as deeply as possible, up to my shoulders (wetting my sweater), and, with fist tightly clasped around a wad of leaves, saw the toes of the frog. After carefully extracting the frog from the leaves, I held it gently but firmly, swished it in the water to clean it, and then turned it over and over, looking at all the parts of a frog that make it a wonderful creature. My heart swelled as a child . . . not from pride for having successfully captured the frog . . . but rather from being there alone with the frog, the stream, the moss, rocks, and earth, sensing something powerful, something ethereal, envelop me in a mystical vapor . . . and I felt myself linked to ancient ones whose voices seemed to drift among the trees and across the water.

It was my first foray across the bridges into vespers . . . into a realm of stillness, a quiet so deep, so powerful, so thick that breathing and heartbeats slow, ushering transcendence that envelopes the world around me and within . . . simultaneously generating sojourns of openness and reflection, sometimes shared but most often experienced alone, where the most beautiful of thoughts swirl in synchrony with a celestial cadence. Within my vespers, energies swell and mingle . . . and there is peace.

My vespers send me racing across time and space to something I reach out for but cannot hold. My vespers do not incorporate prayers in the traditional sense. Few if any words are spoken aloud or within during my vespers. The linkages, the communications, the messages, are beyond words. And yet the vespers I've experienced leave no doubt regarding a shared passage with God.

As I reflect on my vespers and the bridges that lead to them, themes radiate out like a fan in different modes and categories. Some reflect special days hunting, fishing, or just rambling about. Others reflect special places or special times, or encounters with special people doing special things. Some evoke sadness, fear, and humility. Others resurrect joy, wonder, and euphoria. Collectively, they are woven together to become like a song . . . the song of a mortal's pilgrimage. And I've learned that there are no end points.

Rather I've found that the bridges to vespers, the journeys, the processes are themselves hallowed ground, and that the vespers revealed by the bridges are fluid . . . flowing together with ever deepening currents.

Some of my vespers in the outdoors over the years, and the bridges that led me to them, took my life to near perfection, if only for precious moments. There was a special frosty December morning during my high school days in Arkansas when my beloved setter, Molly, came down on a rock-solid gorgeous point alongside a fencerow bordering a soybean field. As the covey rose, I dropped three quail with three separate, deliberate shots . . . and . . . the event was witnessed by friends.

As a Boy Scout camping with my troop on a sand bar along the lower White River in Arkansas, I drifted away from camp one October morning in the predawn quiet and the fog, surrounded by the forest primeval, and shot a gray squirrel an hour or so later at forty yards with a borrowed .22 rifle as the squirrel jumped from one tree to another and was airborne . . . an event witnessed only by me (and I still can't believe I did it, and I suspect neither did the squirrel).

There was a special doe shot on my farm in Mississippi in the golden glow of a January afternoon that was so quiet that I could hear robins turning leaves on the pasture in front of me. After field dressing the doe, I sat on the ground beside her, stroking her, prayers of thanksgiving drifting from my heart and lips until darkness settled over the landscape.

One of my most cherished vespers occurred alongside a deep pool of a river near Sitka, Alaska, as a couple of huge Coho salmon tried to pull my young sons from the cobblestone riverbank they were standing on . . . and almost succeeded in doing it before the boys were grabbed, each in his turn, by their belts and held in place by me. The salmon were landed by the boys, and we walked together over two miles with the fish through Alaskan rainforest full of moss and huge trees to beat a low tide that would have beached our boat.

One cold March afternoon there was a golden eagle in the Ozarks that soared across fold upon fold of gray winter hills as I looked *down* on it and a green thread of a river from my vantage point on a high, rocky bluff. The quiet that surrounded the eagle and me was beyond imagining . . . just as it was one July evening on the Archie Fork of the Little Red River in the hills near Leslie, Arkansas, when, as a boy in my teens, light spinning rod in hand, I waded slowly from riffle to pool, riffle to pool, casting for smallmouth bass as wood thrushes filled the darkening forest with flute calls . . . the bass coming from the emerald clear water like bronze jewels. Then I turned and saw a locally known and protected fugitive from the law sitting on the stream bank watching me. He was a man who had, over his years in solitude and isolation, evolved into a hermit, trapper, and sheep herder of some legend. Although I'd been told he had committed murder (revenge in a courtroom for a murdered friend as I recall), I just looked at him, unafraid, waiting. He smiled and then suggested without words that the bass I had just caught and was preparing to put on my stringer should be returned to the river. I looked at the bass, saw something beautiful beyond words in the fish, the river, and the man, released the fish, and, turning again, saw that the man had vanished. From that day forward, after catching literally thousands of smallmouth bass, I've never kept another.

Images of days spent hunting snow geese on a rice irrigation reservoir (and never getting a single shot!), pass-shooting ducks over minnow ponds, and calling crows on a clear midwinter afternoon in the hills . . . all with my lifelong friend Don Flynn . . . rush through my heart in a way that lets me know that there was a third participant always present. Say what you will, but I'm convinced that God walks in the woods and fields and on the water when friends are together hunting and fishing.

There are vespers associated with ramblings: the way lights twinkled in a distant village on the shore of a lake at sunset in the Dominican Republic . . . and I just stood there on the mountaintop with my gorgeous new bride from Panama, both of us having just climbed to the top, with me carrying on my shoulders the outboard motor we'd used that day while working on the lake, and feeling stronger than I'd ever felt in my life; the glow of an autumn sunset on a Nepalese hamlet high in the Himalayas, all shadow and soft pastels and quiet among the snowy peaks; the predawn light filtering through thick ocean air in Hong Kong before the city started its day; the calls to prayer for the faithful at sunset in Kuala Lumpur, Mombassa, and Karachi; the soft padding of elephant's feet on cobblestone in Katmandu near a Hindu temple at sunrise; the drift of a Buddhist monk in Cambodia as he went from door to door with his rice bowl; the bugle of an elk one afternoon in the Colorado Rockies, reverberating in my heart and mind all night long, and then locating him the next morning and spending two days packing him out of the mountains to the cabin; the dawn calls of gibbons in Malaysia and howler monkeys in Panama as I threaded my way along jungle trails; the rush of the sea and wind as I stood watch on vessels plying oceans from the tropics to the sub-arctic; the roar of surf in Puerto Rico as I sipped the morning's first cup of hot coffee, watched the coming of dawn, and prepared my tackle for some tarpon fishing on local lagoons; the ghost images of barn owls in the predawn darkness during my morning runs in the streets of Santo

Domingo and along the rocky coast; the awesome vastness of the Serengeti escarpment in Kenya after a thunderstorm, with the sun exploding on clouds as the land exploded with life; the rich music of a Slavic band in a tiny restaurant on a spit of land jutting out in a lake on the Yugoslavian-Albanian border, and the equally rich wine and wonderful conversation with my Montenegro colleagues as we discussed values and fisheries and the prospects of the inevitable civil war (which came the following year); encountering a mystic holy man under a tree while trekking to the Anapurna Sanctuary, exchanging a pair of jeans with him for a prayer wheel he offered, and only later realizing that the well-worn shaft was made from a human femur, the spindle from the tusk of a deer thought to be extinct, and the enclosed prayers written in a language that is fading from the world . . . the man spoke with me in that language, slowly and deliberately, with penetrating eyes and mind, and, through some power of exchange I cannot explain, I understood every word; sloshing in the darkness of a dreary night in Kampala and finding a young girl perhaps fourteen or fifteen years old sitting in the rain with a newborn child . . . and so longing to take the child from her and give it a life in another world . . . and knowing that I could not do it and that the child likely would not live through the night . . . giving the little girl a soft touch, a smile, and some money . . . then walking on in the darkness, my tears blending with the mist and drizzle around me; caught in a terrible storm on the Kapuas River one night in Borneo, thunder crashing all around, the little boat churning downstream, with lightning flashes the only light to show the way . . . knowing that we had to travel on to the settlement more than thirty miles away, but also knowing that doing so in the darkness and in the storm and in the surging currents of the river could lead to our death, by drowning, by crocodiles, or both; listening to the chattering of ptarmigan while hunting them in the snowy hills northeast of Fairbanks, stalking them at 20 degrees below zero, freezing one side of my nose and face, hungry from hard trekking on the hunt because the cheese sandwich I'd made and placed in my hunting coat pocket was made of stone, and then realizing that I didn't want to be anywhere else doing anything else, that I'd never been happier; caught in a traffic jam in a crowded bus in Kuala Lumpur, with rain pouring down, the windows of the bus up, and personal space ending at my skin . . . and laughing . . . and the laughter catching among the Malaysians on the bus . . . all of us laughing at the ridiculous situation we were in, transforming misery to humor, and me realizing at that moment that we can choose to be happy or choose to be sad . . . that the choice starts inside us and is not dictated to us by the world around us; witnessing a mother grizzly bear fighting a huge male grizzly out in the middle of an icy glacial stream (and winning the fight!) while her two cubs scrambled up the hillside away from the river (*and towards me!*), and me scrambling to find another place to watch the drama . . . understanding very clearly and in no uncertain terms, from seeing the fight, that the most dangerous ground on earth is between a mother (of any species) and her "cubs"; holding my infant son in my arms on the back porch of my mother-in-law's home in Panama on a Christmas morning, looking through the mesh of a fence and across a ditch to a young Panamanian mother holding *her* infant son . . . the father of one infant and the mother of another infant looking at each other across impossible barriers and both of us knowing, without speaking a word, that opportunity in life can be an accident of birth; walking with my mother on rural roads in Kentucky, Missouri, Arkansas, Malaysia, Mississippi, Alaska, and England, the common denominator of poetry and spirit of life shared weaving an eternal thread of love and understanding; drifting through a botanical garden with my wife one early spring morning in Warsaw, watching old men and pigeons and young couples with children . . . surrounded by the essence of new life and new opportunity in an old country; the call of breeding wood frogs, the southernmost colony of the species, coming from a remote pond high in the Boston Mountains of north Arkansas on a February night . . . walking alone in those hills at 2:00 a.m., listening as coyotes and great horned owls proclaimed the beautiful, sweet lonesomeness of the place and hour, following the frog calls wherever they led, searching for the pond and the frogs and for my soul, feeling a chill course through me that did not come from the winter winds; walking with my daughter on the gravel beach of an island near Juneau, looking at tide pools while hunting blacktail deer, marveling together at the diversity of life in the pools, then returning to our cabin among the spruces for an evening with dear friends around a wood-burning stove; paddling at night on a huge Canadian lake in a canoe with my father, riding the swells and marveling at the deepness of the sky and the deepness of our love for each other, assimilating his story in my heart for safe keeping; the hugs I got from my sisters when I came home from two years in Southeast Asia; sitting beside one of them throughout a very long night, deep in prayer for her healing, and waking while shadows in the room were still deep, her hand squeezing mine, to find the prayers answered; sharing beautiful days with my other sister as we explored the land and people of her dreams and her realizing finally that she has always been my personal princess; fishing the Little Missouri River in the Ouachita Mountains of Southwest Arkansas with my brother when the smallmouth bass were ripping up every top-water lure we threw at them; sitting in a mountain tea shop on a drizzly night in northern Sumatra while tiny, tasseled horses pulled taxi carts on cobblestone streets and the streetlights of candles rather than electric giving the village all the look and feel of something from a Charles Dickens novel . . . and the wonderful talk with a particularly wonderful young man, a poet, back when speaking Bahasa was as easy for me as speaking English . . . spicy tea and conversation warming both body and spirit . . . each of us knowing that we'd never see each other again, but knowing we'd be in each other's lives forever; the sound of a social ballad, "Bridge over Troubled Waters," echoing across a university campus on a Sunday afternoon in the spring of my freshman year . . . and now hearing it across the years and confirming what I knew then—that bridges are catalysts for discernment of truth, and that beyond truth is knowledge, and that beyond knowledge is wisdom, and that beyond wisdom is God.

I pause now as I write. Vesper songs surround me. Their echoes come to me from sources both known and unknown . . . on spiritual winds . . . swirling with conflict, conquest, love, caring, adventure, exploration, discovery, compassion, loss, sadness, hope, mercy, reflection, and prayer . . . the essences of life. Spatial and temporal dimensions really do not matter very much. The bridges formed by the vesper songs transcend the mortal realms. Kinship is universal.

Bolstered by faith, we discover that the wonder, the currents, the grandeur, the light, and the revelations from our vespers can be projected with courage beyond time and space and blood, into and through the consciousness of others, and on into the highest realms of the human oversoul, with a degree of honesty and purity and power and depth that absolutely and completely melds us across generations, cultures, and civilizations. Truly we *are* one in spirit, one in God.

In sharing our vespers, we discover that the compass bearing of kindred sojourners is confirmed, the steps of our pilgrimages coalesce and are strengthened, and our collective chorus is tuned and packaged for passage and transfer. Then, when time stops for us, and matter no longer exists or can even be defined, when energy has been transformed from the physical to the spiritual, the vespers we've shared may well be our most enduring gifts to those who follow. For us all they become bridges of immortality.